THE VANISHING HEIRESS

The Unsolved Disappearance of Dorothy Arnold

SHADOWS OF THE PAST
BOOK I

ELIZA HAWTHORNE

TABLE OF CONTENTS

INTRODUCTION

On a cold day in December 1910, Dorothy Arnold left her family's home on the Upper East Side of New York City and vanished without a trace. She was a young socialite, the daughter of a wealthy perfume importer, and she had all the world at her feet. Her disappearance was as sudden as it was mystifying, leaving her family and the public grasping for answers that would never come. The streets of New York buzzed with rumors, the newspapers trumpeted headlines, and private detectives scoured the city, but Dorothy Arnold was nowhere to be found. The emotional impact of her absence was profound, leaving a void in the hearts of those who knew her.

Dorothy's story is not just a tale of a missing person. It is a window into the world of early 20th-century New York, a city teeming with ambition, secrets, and societal pressures. Dorothy, a young woman with dreams of her own, was not a mere heiress. She aspired to become a writer and break free from the expectations placed upon her by her wealthy family. Her disappearance, shrouded in mystery, opens up a labyrinth of questions. What happened to Dorothy Arnold on that fateful day? Was it a crime, an escape, or something else entirely? This is a story that will make you feel the weight of societal expectations and the struggle for individuality, a struggle that Dorothy faced every day.

This book, "The Vanishing Heiress: The Unsolved Disappearance of Dorothy Arnold," is the first in the Shadows of the Past series. It offers a unique blend of historical narrative and true crime mystery, shedding light on the darker corners of history. Each book in the series will combine meticulous research with vivid storytelling, aiming to captivate history buffs, true crime readers, and anyone fascinated by the societal and media influences on crime narratives.

Our purpose here is twofold. First, we aim to immerse you in the mystery of Dorothy Arnold's disappearance using factual research and immersive storytelling. You will walk with her through the streets of New York, feel her dreams and fears, and experience the societal pressures she faced. Second, we will provide educational insight into early 20th-century crime-solving techniques, societal norms, and the media's role in shaping public perception. This is a journey that will stimulate your intellect and broaden your understanding of historical crime narratives, offering a unique perspective on the societal and media influences on crime narratives.

The book will cover various aspects of Dorothy Arnold's life and disappearance. We will start with her background—her personal life, her ambitions, and the social pressures she faced. Using witness accounts and tracing her last known steps, we will then recreate the day she vanished. The investigation that followed will be examined in detail, comparing the methods used then with those of modern forensics. We will also delve into the Arnold family's dynamics, their secrecy, and the impact of their wealth on the investigation. The role of the media will be explored, showing how the case was portrayed and how societal views on women influenced public perception. Finally, we will analyze various theories about what might have happened to Dorothy, from a botched abortion to a planned escape.

This journey aims to humanize Dorothy Arnold. She was not just a name in a headline but a young woman with hopes and dreams. Her disappearance had a profound impact on her family, who were left to grapple with uncertainty and loss. By exploring this case, we hope to foster an emotional connection and stimulate critical thinking about the unsolved aspects and expert analysis. We will reflect on how society shapes crime narratives, particularly regarding women and wealth. You will feel the emotional weight carried by those left behind and the impact of Dorothy's absence on their lives.

Dear reader, I invite you to join me in this investigation. Let us walk the streets of early 20th-century New York together. Let us uncover the layers of this mystery and feel the emotional weight carried by those left behind. This is not just a story to be read; it is a puzzle to be solved, a journey to be undertaken.

The adventure awaits.

CHAPTER 1
THE WORLD OF DOROTHY ARNOLD

November 30, 1910

"It seems that every day, I am reminded of the limits placed upon me by my family and society. While I walk among them, I feel the weight of expectations that have nothing to do with who I am but only with the life they expect me to live. Must I forever be seen as merely an heiress and not as a person with dreams of my own?"

On the morning of December 12, 1910, Dorothy Arnold, dressed in her finest blue serge coat and black velvet hat, prepared for a day in Manhattan. She was a familiar figure in New York's high society, known for her grace and ambition. Yet beneath the polished exterior lay a young woman yearning for more than the gilded cage her status afforded her. Her disappearance would soon grip the city, exposing the interplay of wealth, societal expectations, and the relentless pursuit of independence.

Dorothy Arnold grew up in an era of unparalleled opulence and stark social contrasts. As the daughter of Francis Arnold, a prominent perfume importer, her life was a testament to the extravagance of the Gilded Age. She resided in a grand mansion on the Upper East Side, surrounded by luxury and privilege. Her home, adorned with fine art and exquisite furnishings, was a sanctuary from the bustling city streets. Lavish estates in the countryside provided a retreat for the family's summer months, offering a glimpse into a world reserved for the elite.

Her education, a reflection of her family's wealth and status, was a double-edged sword. Dorothy attended exclusive private schools, where she received the finest instruction in literature, languages, and the arts. These institutions not only prepared her for the social duties expected of her but also fueled her intellectual curiosity. However, the more she learned, the more she felt the constraints of her societal role, yearning for a life beyond the expectations of marriage and social propriety. Her struggle for independence was a constant battle against the norms of her time.

The contradiction gnawed at her. She felt the weight of her family's expectations pressing down, a constant reminder that her ambitions were, in their eyes, impractical—perhaps even impossible. Her father's voice echoed in her mind: *"A writer? That's not a serious pursuit for a woman of your standing."* She smiled through the endless debutante balls and charity events, hiding her frustration behind a façade of grace, but her private journal told a different story, one filled with her innermost thoughts and desires.

High-society events and galas were a staple of Dorothy's life. She attended countless soirées, debutante balls, and charity events, each one a dazzling display of wealth and power. These gatherings were more than social occasions; they were arenas where alliances were forged and reputations were built. Dorothy moved effortlessly through these circles, yet the glittering facade often masked a deeper sense of isolation. Amid the sparkling chandeliers and elegant gowns, she struggled with the rigid expectations placed upon her.

"Another evening, another charade," Dorothy often thought as she passed through the grand ballrooms, her face adorned with the practiced smile of a dutiful daughter. The relentless weight of high society's expectations sat heavily on her shoulders. She longed for something more—something real, beyond the glittering trappings of her station.

The Gilded Age was a period marked by an economic boom and the rise of industrial magnates. Figures like John Jacob Astor, Cornelius Vanderbilt, and Andrew Carnegie dominated the social landscape, their wealth and influence shaping the fabric of New York City. The era's opulence was matched only by its social stratification, where status and reputation were paramount. For families like the Arnolds, maintaining their position in society was a relentless endeavor, fraught with pressure and scrutiny.

Despite her privileged upbringing, Dorothy faced significant limitations imposed by societal norms. Women of her class were expected to marry well, uphold family honor, and engage in charitable work. Career opportunities were scarce, and ambitions beyond the domestic sphere were often stifled. Dorothy's desire to become a writer clashed with these expectations. She penned several short stories and sought publication, only to face rejection and discouragement from her father, who deemed her aspirations frivolous. The weight of these societal expectations was a constant burden on Dorothy.

The rejection letters from publishers were piling up. Dorothy could recall the words in each letter—cruel reminders that her creativity was not valued in a society where women of her class were only seen as future wives and mothers. Still, every evening, she scribbled furiously into her notebook by candlelight, the pages filled with her secret rebellion against the life she had been told to embrace.

"You are not just a name in society, Dorothy," she would remind herself, staring into the mirror before each social event. *"You are more than that. You have a voice, a mind."* But how long could she keep up the charade before she either lost herself or found a way out?

The tension within the Arnold family only grew as days turned into weeks. Whispers of unease filled the mansion as each family member dealt with Dorothy's absence differently. Mary's nights became plagued by worry, Elsie withdrew into a world of silent guilt, and Francis, ever the patriarch, struggled to maintain control over a situation spiraling into chaos.

Each family member dealt with Dorothy's absence differently. Francis's sense of control was shaken, and Mary's maternal instincts pushed her toward despair. Elsie, however, struggled with guilt and an overwhelming need to contribute to the search. She became her mother's support while also feeling the weight of her sister's secrets. These internal tensions became as much a part of the family's daily life as the investigation itself, showing how deeply the disappearance shaped their emotional landscapes.

FAMILY TIES: THE ARNOLDS' SOCIAL STANDING

Francis Arnold's internal struggle became increasingly evident as Dorothy's ambitions grew. A man accustomed to control, he found his world unraveling with her disappearance. The looming public scandal and the uncertainty gnawed at him, leading to his decision to maintain silence, even with law enforcement. This choice created friction at home, straining the family's relationships and compounding their grief. The weight of his choices led to a household fraught with tension, each member grappling with the impact of Dorothy's absence.

The last few weeks before Dorothy vanished had been especially fraught. Their conversations had become more strained, Dorothy's once polite deference giving way to flashes of rebellion. *"Why is it so wrong for me to want more?"* she had once snapped at the breakfast table, her voice trembling with the frustration that had been building for years.

"Your place is here," her father responded curtly, not even bothering to look up from his newspaper. *"You have everything a young woman could ask for."* But Dorothy knew that the life her father imagined for her was a gilded cage.

Elsie Arnold, Dorothy's younger sister, bore her own burden. She was not just a sibling but a confidante, privy to Dorothy's deepest hopes and fears. Dorothy had confided in Elsie about her struggles with societal expectations and her yearning for independence. In the wake of Dorothy's disappearance, Elsie was consumed with guilt and isolation. She questioned whether she had missed any signs, any clues that could have prevented the tragedy. As the public speculated and the media swirled around their story, Elsie retreated further into the oppressive silence of the family mansion, carrying the weight of Dorothy's secrets alone.

The days following Dorothy's disappearance brought Elsie no peace. The whispers of the city echoed inside the mansion, every visitor offering condolences laced with gossip. Could she have known? Could she have stopped her sister from making a desperate escape? These were questions that haunted Elsie's every waking moment, and every unanswered one weighed more heavily than the last.

Even the most well-hidden secrets would soon face the harsh scrutiny of New York's relentless media, setting the stage for a scandal that would grip the nation.

THE INTRICATE WORLD OF DOROTHY ARNOLD

This chapter delves into the intricate world of Dorothy Arnold, a young woman caught between the gilded splendor of her upbringing and the suffocating constraints of her era. Her story is one of ambition, struggle, and the desperate search for freedom in a world that offered little room for deviation. As you walk through the halls of the Arnold mansion and the bustling streets of early 20th-century New York, you will uncover the layers of a life marked by privilege and pain, mystery and longing.

The Arnold family stood as a pillar of high society in early 20th-century New York. Francis Arnold, Dorothy's father, was a man whose business acumen had elevated the family to the upper echelons of social standing. His perfume business was not just successful; it was a symbol of affluence and taste that permeated the family's identity. Francis's ventures extended beyond perfumes, with investments in real estate and other enterprises that secured their financial stability and social prominence. This wealth created an environment where Dorothy and her siblings were afforded every privilege, but it also placed them under immense scrutiny.

The Arnold lineage was one of distinction and influence. The family's history was filled with connections to notable figures and institutions, creating a network of relationships that bolstered their standing. Dorothy's uncle, a Supreme Court justice, added a layer of prestige that few families could claim. These connections were not merely social; they were instrumental in shaping public perception and the efforts to find Dorothy after her disappearance. The weight of the Arnold name carried significant influence in New York's social circles, where maintaining appearances and reputation was paramount.

Francis Arnold's success in the perfume industry was a cornerstone of the family's wealth. His ability to secure lucrative contracts and expand the business demonstrated his sharp business mind. The perfumes he imported were sought after by the elite, and his company became synonymous with luxury and sophistication. Beyond perfumes, Francis invested in various ventures, including real estate, which further solidified the family's financial foundation. His business dealings were marked by shrewdness and a relentless drive for success, qualities that defined his approach to both business and family life.

The Arnold family's connections extended deep into New York's elite. They rubbed shoulders with the Astors, the Vanderbilts, and other titans of industry. These relationships were nurtured at exclusive clubs and society events, where alliances were formed, and social standing was both displayed and reinforced. The Metropolitan Club, the Union Club, and other elite establishments were regular haunts for Francis

Arnold and his peers. These venues were more than social gathering spots; they were places where business deals were struck and social hierarchies were maintained. The Arnolds were a fixture in these circles, their presence a testament to their status.

Prominent family, friends, and associates played crucial roles in the Arnolds' social life. The family was often seen at the most prestigious events, from lavish parties to cultural gatherings at the Metropolitan Museum of Art. These interactions were not just about socializing; they were about maintaining the intricate web of relationships that upheld their status. The Arnolds' participation in elite social clubs provided them with opportunities to influence and be influenced by the movers and shakers of their time. These connections were invaluable, especially when Dorothy disappeared, and the family needed to leverage every relationship to aid in the search.

The Arnold family's social standing shaped every aspect of Dorothy's life. It dictated the schools she attended, the people she associated with, and the expectations placed upon her. This standing also influenced the investigation into her disappearance. The family's wealth and connections meant that no resource was spared in the search efforts. Private detectives were hired, and the case received extensive media coverage, partly because of the family's prominence. The public was captivated by the mystery of a young socialite vanishing, and the Arnold name ensured that the case remained in the spotlight.

For Francis Arnold, the disappearance of his daughter was more than a personal tragedy; it was a threat to the family's legacy. His business success and social standing had always been intertwined with his identity and his control over the family. The uncertainty of Dorothy's fate was a blow to his meticulously crafted world. The pressure to maintain a facade of composure while grappling with the unknown took a toll on him and the entire family. The Arnolds were used to being in control and exerting influence, but Dorothy's disappearance exposed the limits of their power.

In the weeks and months following Dorothy's disappearance, the family's connections were both a blessing and a curse. While they provided avenues to explore in the search, they also subjected the family to relentless public scrutiny. The media, eager for any detail about the missing heiress, descended upon the Arnolds, turning their private anguish into a public spectacle. The family's social standing, which had once been a source of pride, became a double-edged sword, amplifying their suffering and complicating their efforts to find Dorothy.

The Arnold family's place in society was a defining feature of their existence, shaping their actions and reactions in times of both prosperity and crisis. Their wealth, connections, and influence created a world of privilege for Dorothy, but it also imposed rigid expectations and intense pressure. Francis Arnold's success in business and the family's prominent social ties played pivotal roles in the unfolding drama of Dorothy's disappearance, illustrating how deeply intertwined personal and public lives can become in the glare of high society.

A DAY IN THE LIFE OF DOROTHY ARNOLD

Dorothy Arnold's days began with a sense of routine that belied the turbulence she felt inside. Each morning, she awoke in her elegantly furnished bedroom, the sunlight filtering through heavy drapes adorned with intricate patterns. Her maid would bring a breakfast tray laden with fresh fruit, pastries, and tea. As she dined, Dorothy often read the morning paper, her mind wandering between current events and her own aspirations. She would then dress for the day, selecting from a wardrobe filled with the latest fashions. Each piece of clothing was a testament to her social standing, carefully chosen to reflect her family's wealth and her own refined taste.

Yet, even in these quiet moments, the weight of her frustrations and desires stirred within her. As she stood before the mirror, carefully pinning her hair, Dorothy often wondered how long she could maintain the facade. What good were these elaborate gowns and parties if she felt hollow inside?

The mornings were often reserved for social engagements or leisurely activities. Dorothy frequently visited the city's most fashionable shops, browsing through the latest collections of dresses, hats, and accessories. Shopping was not just a pastime; it was a statement of her status and a way to assert her individuality within the confines of societal expectations. She also spent considerable time in bookstores, her fingers tracing the spines of newly published works. Reading was a passion that provided a temporary escape from the rigid structures of her life. Her interest in literature extended to writing, and she often carried a notebook, jotting down ideas for stories and essays as she moved through the city.

But even the words on the pages seemed out of reach, Dorothy thought, running her fingers along the spines of freshly published novels. She would glance around the bookstore, watching men freely browse and purchase books while she, though raised to be just as knowledgeable, was expected to enjoy these works without the serious ambition of creating her own.

Afternoons were typically filled with social interactions, a crucial aspect of maintaining her place in high society. Dorothy attended luncheons and teas at the homes of friends and acquaintances, where conversations flowed as freely as the tea. These gatherings were more than social niceties; they were opportunities to forge alliances and maintain one's social network. Dorothy's charm and wit made her a popular guest, yet she often felt the weight of unspoken expectations. She navigated these interactions with grace, aware that every word and gesture was being scrutinized.

"Another luncheon," Dorothy would think, smiling politely as the women around her discussed their latest purchases, engagements, and social plans. They can't imagine how stifling it all feels.

Evenings were reserved for cultural events, a staple of New York's high society. Dorothy was a frequent attendee at the theater and opera, where the city's elite gathered to see and be seen. These events were grand affairs held in opulent venues that mirrored the extravagance of the era. Dorothy reveled in the performances, finding solace in the arts. Yet, even in these moments of enjoyment, she was acutely aware of the societal pressures that dictated her presence there. The theater and opera were not just entertainment; they were arenas where social hierarchies were both displayed and reinforced.

Dorothy's hobbies and interests were a blend of the expected and the personal. Fashion and shopping were public displays of her status, but reading and writing were deeply personal pursuits. She found joy in the written word, both as a reader and a writer. Though she faced rejection in her attempts to get published, she persisted, driven by a desire to carve out a space for herself beyond her social identity. Her writing was a reflection of her inner world, filled with characters and scenarios that resonated with her own struggles for independence and self-expression.

Her social interactions extended beyond formal events. Dorothy often met friends for casual lunches and intimate gatherings, where the conversation was less about social standing and more about personal connections—these moments provided a respite from the constant scrutiny, allowing her to be herself, if only for a short while. Her friendships were a mix of genuine bonds and strategic alliances, each one contributing to her complex social web.

Dorothy's private thoughts and struggles were often captured in her personal writings. She kept a diary where she poured out her frustrations, dreams, and reflections on the world around her. In one entry, she wrote about her desire to break free from societal expectations, expressing a longing for independence that seemed just out of reach. She questioned the roles imposed upon her, wondering if there was more to life than the path laid out by her family and society.

"Will they ever see me for who I really am?"

She had written in one particularly frustrated entry.

"Or will I forever remain the ornament they've created?"

These writings reveal a young woman caught between two worlds: the opulent but confining life of a Gilded Age socialite and the tantalizing but uncertain possibilities of personal freedom. Dorothy's reflections on societal expectations highlight the inner conflict that defined her existence. She yearned to be more than a decorative figure at social events, to have her voice heard and her talents recognized. Yet, the pressures of her social standing and the limitations placed on women of her class made these aspirations difficult to achieve.

When we examine a typical day in Dorothy Arnold's life, we see not just the routines and activities that filled her hours but the deeper currents of ambition, frustration, and yearning that defined her. Her life was a delicate balance of public appearances and private dreams, each day a testament to the complexities of navigating high society as a young woman with aspirations that transcended her prescribed role.

HIGH SOCIETY AND SOCIALITE CULTURE IN 1910

Early 20th-century New York was a city of contrasts, where the shimmer of high society masked the struggles of those beneath its gilded surface. The streets were alive with the clatter of horse-drawn carriages and the hum of new automobiles, each vying for space amongst the throngs of pedestrians. The social elite, however, moved in a world apart, where fashion was both a statement and a weapon in the unspoken war for status. Women like Dorothy Arnold wore the latest styles from Paris, with elaborate hats, tailored dresses, and delicate gloves. These garments were more than just clothing; they were symbols of wealth and taste, markers of one's place in the intricate social hierarchy.

The societal norms of the time dictated a rigid code of conduct, particularly for women of Dorothy's standing. They were expected to be paragons of virtue, embodying grace, poise, and unwavering propriety. Social events were arenas where these qualities were displayed and judged. Debutante balls, charity galas, and exclusive soirées were the stages upon which the social elite performed their roles. Each event was meticulously orchestrated, from the guest list to the floral arrangements, reflecting the host's status and influence.

These gatherings were not mere social functions; they were battlegrounds where reputations were made or broken.

Maintaining a good reputation was crucial for families like the Arnolds. Social standing influenced every aspect of their lives, from marriage prospects to business dealings. A family's name was its most valuable asset, and any hint of scandal could have devastating consequences. Marriages were often strategic alliances designed to consolidate wealth and power. For a young woman like Dorothy, her future was intertwined with the family's social standing. Her actions, her associations, and even her appearance all had to align with the expectations of high society. Any deviation could jeopardize not only her prospects but also her family's reputation.

The roles and expectations for women in high society were particularly stringent. From a young age, they were trained to embody the ideals of the "True Woman," a paragon of domesticity, piety, and submission. Their education, while extensive, was often geared towards preparing them for their roles as wives and mothers. Personal freedoms were limited, and career opportunities were scarce. Women were expected to uphold family honor and engage in charitable work, but their ambitions beyond the domestic sphere were often stifled. The societal pressure to conform was immense, and the cost of defiance could be severe.

Dorothy Arnold was acutely aware of these pressures. Her life was a constant balancing act between her personal desires and the expectations placed upon her. The socialite culture of the time influenced every aspect of her existence, from her daily routines to her deepest aspirations. The weight of maintaining her family's reputation weighed heavily on her, shaping her actions and decisions. Her desire to become a writer was seen as a frivolous pursuit, incompatible with her social role. Yet, this ambition was a core part of her identity, a silent rebellion against the constraints of her world.

These cultural norms also colored the public's perception of Dorothy's disappearance. The media portrayed her as the quintessential socialite, a young woman whose life was defined by privilege and luxury. This narrative, however, overlooked the complexities of her reality. The societal pressures, the limited personal freedoms, the struggle for independence—these were the unseen forces that shaped her life. These perceptions influenced the investigation into her disappearance, with assumptions and biases clouding the search for the truth.

In many ways, Dorothy's story is a reflection of the broader societal dynamics of early 20th-century New York. The socialite culture, with its rigid expectations and relentless scrutiny, created an environment where appearances were paramount, and deviations were not tolerated. Dorothy's disappearance exposed the fragility of this world, revealing the cracks beneath the polished surface. Her story is not just a mystery to be solved; it is a window into a society grappling with the tensions between tradition and change, privilege and aspiration.

As we explore the intricacies of Dorothy's life and the world she inhabited, we gain a deeper understanding of the forces that shaped her fate. Her story is a poignant reminder of the personal struggles hidden behind the facade of high society, a testament to the resilience of those who dared to dream beyond their prescribed roles.

THE SOCIETAL PRESSURES OF BEING A SOCIALITE

Dorothy Arnold's life was a delicate dance, choreographed by the societal expectations that governed every move she made. As a young woman in high society, she faced immense pressure to marry within her social class. Her parents, particularly her father, expected her to secure a match that would not only uphold but also enhance the family's status. Suitors were scrutinized not just for their character but for their lineage and wealth. This pressure to marry well was relentless, a constant reminder that her worth was tied to her ability to form an advantageous union.

The expectations extended beyond marriage. Dorothy was also tasked with upholding the family's reputation in every aspect of her life. Her behavior, her associations, and even her appearance were all under constant surveillance. Any misstep could bring scandal and shame, not just upon her but upon her entire family. This need to conform to social norms was suffocating, leaving little room for personal expression or deviation from the prescribed path. The weight of these expectations pressed heavily upon Dorothy, shaping her actions and limiting her choices.

The psychological impact of these pressures was profound. Dorothy often felt isolated and suffocated by the demands placed upon her. The constant scrutiny and the rigid expectations created an environment where she could rarely let her guard down. Her personal ambitions, particularly her desire to become a writer, were seen as frivolous and incompatible with her social role. The tension between her aspirations and the expectations placed upon her created a sense of inner conflict and frustration. She longed for independence, for a life where she could pursue her dreams without the constraints of societal norms.

Dorothy's experience was not unique. Many socialites of her time faced similar pressures, their lives dictated by the same rigid expectations. Consuelo Vanderbilt, for instance, was famously forced into a marriage with the Duke of Marlborough, a union arranged to elevate her family's status. Despite her own desires, Consuelo had little say in the matter, her life shaped by the ambitions of her parents. Similarly, Alice Roosevelt, the daughter of President Theodore Roosevelt, struggled with the expectations placed upon her as a member of the political elite. Her rebellious spirit often clashed with societal norms, earning her both admiration and criticism.

Societal reactions to women who defied these norms were often harsh —those who dared to step outside the prescribed roles faced ostracism and scandal. Edith Wharton, a renowned writer of the time, used her literary talents to critique the very society she was a part of. Her works, filled with keen observations on the constraints faced by women, resonated with many but also drew criticism from those who saw her as a threat to the status quo. These examples illustrate that Dorothy's struggles were part of a broader pattern, reflective of the societal dynamics of the time.

The societal pressures Dorothy faced may have played a significant role in her disappearance. The relentless demands to conform, the lack of personal freedom, and the oppressive expectations could have driven her to seek an escape. Theories abound about what might have happened to her, but one plausible scenario is that she chose to flee from the constraints of her life. The desire for independence, coupled with the fear of failing to meet societal expectations, could have propelled her to take drastic measures. Psychological theories suggest that prolonged exposure to such pressures can lead to feelings of desperation and a need to break free, even if it means leaving everything behind.

Analyzing Dorothy's situation through the lens of these societal pressures provides a deeper understanding of her possible motivations. The intersection of personal ambition and societal expectation created a volatile mix, one that could easily lead to a sense of entrapment. The societal norms of the time, which valued reputation and status above individual fulfillment, left little room for deviation. For Dorothy, the desire to escape these constraints may have been a driving force, a desperate bid for a life where she could be true to herself.

As we reflect on Dorothy Arnold's story, we see that her disappearance is not just a mystery to be solved but a poignant reflection of the societal pressures that shaped her life. Her story is a testament to the resilience of those who dared to dream beyond their prescribed roles and a reminder of the personal struggles hidden behind the facade of high society. The societal pressures she faced were immense, shaping every aspect of her life and ultimately contributing to the mystery that continues to captivate us. Dorothy's story speaks to the universal human desire for freedom and self-expression, a desire that transcends time and social boundaries.

CULTURAL AND LITERARY MOVEMENTS OF THE GILDED AGE

Exploring the broader cultural and literary movements, we can see how the works of Edith Wharton and other writers critiqued the constraints faced by women in high society. Edith Wharton's novels, such as The Age of Innocence and The House of Mirth, delved into the intricate web of societal expectations and the limitations placed on women within high society. These works provided a critical examination of the oppressive norms and expectations that governed the lives of women like Dorothy. Wharton's portrayal of the struggles faced by her female characters resonated with many readers and shed light on the pervasive nature of these societal constraints. By examining these literary movements, we gain a deeper understanding of the challenges and pressures that women like Dorothy grappled with in their pursuit of autonomy and self-expression.

In examining the societal norms and gender dynamics of the Gilded Age, it becomes evident that the experiences of women like Edith Wharton's characters were not isolated incidents but rather emblematic of a larger social phenomenon. Women such as Alva Vanderbilt, Consuelo Vanderbilt, and Jennie Jerome, who later became Lady Randolph Churchill, navigated similar societal pressures and constraints as depicted in Wharton's works. Their lives, like those of Wharton's characters, were intricately bound by the expectations and limitations imposed by high society. By drawing parallels between the fictional portrayals in literature and the real-life experiences of prominent socialites, we gain a more comprehensive understanding of the pervasive impact of societal norms on women during the Gilded Age. This nuanced analysis allows us to appreciate the complexities of gender dynamics and social expectations that shaped the lives of women in this era, shedding light on the broader cultural and historical context in which these individuals lived and sought to assert their agency.

CHAPTER 2

THE DAY SHE VANISHED

December 7, 1910

As the days go by, I find myself increasingly suffocated by the confines of societal expectations. It's as if I am expected to play a role that has been assigned to me without any consideration for my own aspirations and desires. The weight of these predetermined paths is heavy, and I long to break free and live a life that is true to myself.

DECEMBER 12, 1910: THE MORNING ROUTINE

On the morning of December 12, 1910, Dorothy Arnold woke up in her family's grand home on the Upper East Side. The mansion was a testament to their wealth, with its high ceilings, elaborate moldings, and richly furnished rooms. As the early winter sun filtered through the heavy drapes, Dorothy stirred from her slumber, little did she know this would be the last morning she would be the last morning she would spend in such opulent surroundings.

She dressed in her elegant nightgown and made her way to the breakfast table, where her family was already gathered.

Dorothy's mornings were usually calm and structured, a reflection of the disciplined household her father, Francis Arnold, maintained. As she sat down to breakfast, the table was adorned with fine china and silverware, a testament to the family's affluence. The meal consisted of fresh fruit, pastries, and tea, prepared meticulously by the household staff. Dorothy engaged in light conversation with her parents and siblings, discussing the day's plans and the latest society gossip. Her father, ever the businessman, read the morning paper, occasionally sharing snippets of news that caught his interest.

After breakfast, Dorothy returned to her room to prepare for her day out in Manhattan. She selected a blue serge coat from her wardrobe, a practical yet stylish choice for the winter weather. The coat was tailored to fit her slender frame, with a high collar and brass buttons that gleamed in the light. She paired it with a black velvet hat adorned with a single feather, a fashionable accessory that completed her ensemble. Her jewelry was understated but elegant—a delicate gold necklace and a pair of pearl earrings, gifts from her parents that she wore with pride.

As Dorothy dressed, she felt a sense of excitement mixed with a hint of apprehension. She was planning to shop for a new dress, a task she relished but also approached with a critical eye. Fashion was important in her social circles, and each new outfit was an opportunity to make a statement. Yet, beneath her cheerful exterior, there were signs of unease. Her family had noticed her restlessness in recent weeks, though she had managed to mask it well. Today, however, there was a sense of resolve in her demeanor, as if she had made a decision that only she knew about.

The tension growing within Dorothy did not go unnoticed by her mother, Mary. She later found herself replaying that morning in her mind, searching for signs that her daughter's determination meant more than just a day of shopping. *"She seemed different,"* Mary recalled, haunted by the fleeting look of determination she noticed in Dorothy's eyes—an expression that, at the time, she had dismissed. Those who saw Dorothy that morning described her mood as cheerful and composed. Her maid, who helped her dress, noted that Dorothy seemed lighter, almost relieved. At the breakfast table, she engaged in conversation with a genuine smile, enthusiastically discussing her plans. There was no sign of distress or unusual behavior, but her mother, Mary Arnold, later remembered that fleeting look of determination. It was a look that Mary would replay in her mind countless times in the days and weeks that followed.

Dorothy's plans for the day were simple. She intended to visit several shops on Fifth Avenue to find a dress for an upcoming social event. Shopping trips were a regular part of her routine, often accompanied by friends or family. However, on this particular day, she chose to go alone, a decision that would later be seen as significant in the context of her disappearance. There was also the possibility of meeting a friend, though no concrete plans had been made. Dorothy enjoyed the freedom of wandering the city, exploring new boutiques, and indulging in the vibrant energy of Manhattan. It was a rare escape from the confines of her structured life.

As Dorothy left her home that morning, she was a vision of poise and elegance. Her blue serge coat and black velvet hat made her stand out in the bustling streets, a beacon of high society amidst the crowds of New York. She walked with purpose, her steps confident and measured, a sight to behold. Yet, beneath the surface, a storm of emotions swirled, hinting at a deeper, unspoken turmoil. This contrast between her outward appearance and inner state would later become a key element in the mystery of her disappearance.

What started as a typical day would soon unravel into one of the most perplexing mysteries of the early 20th century. Dorothy's every move and interaction as she navigated the city would be scrutinized, her routine steps dissected in the quest for clues. The cheerful young woman who left her home that morning would vanish without a trace, leaving behind a trail of unanswered questions and a family in desperate need of closure.

THE SHOPPING TRIP: ERRANDS IN MANHATTAN

Dorothy Arnold stepped out into the crisp December air, her blue serge coat wrapped snugly around her. She made her way to the trolley stop, her footsteps echoing on the cobblestone streets. The trolley arrived with a clatter, and she climbed aboard, finding a seat by the window. The ride to the ferry terminal was a familiar one, the city's skyline unfolding before her as she traveled. The trolley jostled and swayed, its passengers a mix of businessmen, shoppers, and children heading to school.

Upon reaching the ferry terminal, Dorothy disembarked and walked towards the dock. The Hudson River stretched out before her, its waters cold and choppy. She boarded the ferry, the sounds of seagulls and the distant hum of the city in the background. The ferry ride was brief but invigorating, the wind tugging at her hat and bringing a flush to her cheeks. She watched the skyline of Manhattan grow closer, the towering buildings and bustling piers a testament to the city's relentless energy.

Once in Manhattan, Dorothy's first stop was Brentano's bookstore, a haven for literary enthusiasts like herself. The store was a labyrinth of shelves filled with the latest novels, poetry collections, and literary journals. Dorothy browsed the aisles, her fingers trailing over the spines of

books. She picked up a few volumes, their covers promising tales of adventure and romance. A clerk approached her, offering assistance. They engaged in a brief conversation about the latest releases, the clerk noting Dorothy's keen interest in contemporary fiction. She purchased a couple of books, tucking them into her bag with a satisfied smile. This interaction, though seemingly mundane, would later be scrutinized for any clues about her state of mind.

At this moment, Dorothy appeared cheerful, but there was a quiet intensity beneath the surface—one that the clerk would later reflect on, trying to decipher if there had been something more to her visit. *"She was friendly, engaging,"* he'd later recall. *"But now that I think back, there was something in her eyes, like her mind was elsewhere."*

Her next stop was Park & Tilford's, a candy store that was a feast for the senses, with the rich aroma of chocolate and the vibrant colors of candies in glass jars. Dorothy selected an assortment of chocolates, her favorite indulgence, and engaged in a pleasant conversation with the store's clerk. The employee, a young woman with a warm smile, noted Dorothy's cheerful demeanor and impeccable manners. Dorothy paid for her treats and left the store, her spirits lifted by the sweet purchase. Little did she know, this would be one of the last normal interactions she would have before her mysterious disappearance. Her shopping continued as she visited several tailor shops, searching for the perfect dress. She examined fabrics, compared styles, and consulted with tailors about custom fittings. Each shop was a bustling hive of activity, with seamstresses and tailors working diligently on their creations. Dorothy's interactions were polite and precise, her discerning eye evident as she evaluated each option. She left the shops with a few swatches of fabric and plans to return for fittings.

By the time Dorothy was last seen, she had completed her errands and was heading toward her next destination. Her steps were purposeful, and her figure was a familiar sight on the busy streets of Manhattan. As the city continued its relentless pace, Dorothy Arnold seemed to vanish into the very fabric of New York, leaving behind a trail of questions and a legacy of intrigue.

WITNESSES AND THEIR ACCOUNTS

As Dorothy Arnold moved through the bustling avenues of Manhattan on that fateful day, she crossed paths with numerous individuals, each offering fragments of her final known moments. These accounts, collected from shopkeepers and passersby, provide a mosaic of her activities and demeanor, though they also introduce layers of complexity and contradiction.

Shopkeepers remembered her well. At Brentano's bookstore, the clerk recalled Dorothy's enthusiasm as she perused the latest literary offerings. Her discussion about contemporary novels and her purchase of a few selected titles painted the picture of a young woman deeply engaged with her intellectual pursuits. The candy store employee at Park & Tilford's noted her cheerful disposition as she selected chocolates, her face lighting up in a warm smile. Tailors who assisted her in various shops described her as purposeful, examining fabrics and discussing custom fittings with a discerning eye. These observations suggested a woman who was not only at ease but also enjoying her day.

Passersby, too, contributed their observations. They saw a well-dressed young woman, a striking figure in her blue serge coat and black velvet hat, moving with confidence through the busy streets. One witness reported seeing her near the corner of Fifth Avenue and 27th Street, walking briskly as if she had a destination in mind. Another recalled her pausing momentarily, perhaps lost in thought, before continuing on her way. These fleeting glimpses of Dorothy added to the sense of normalcy that characterized her day.

Yet, these recollections took on a new light as time went on. Mary Arnold struggled to reconcile the calm, composed Dorothy that witnesses described with the tension she had noticed at breakfast. Each account, no matter how detailed, only deepened the uncertainty, leaving the family grappling with the question: how could Dorothy have disappeared so suddenly and completely?

However, the credibility of these testimonies varied. Some accounts were consistent, reinforcing the image of Dorothy as composed and cheerful. The bookstore clerk and candy store employee, for instance, provided similar descriptions of her demeanor, bolstering the reliability of their observations. Passersby, who saw her walking along Fifth Avenue, described her attire and behavior in a way that matched the shopkeepers' accounts. Yet, not all testimonies aligned perfectly. One tailor mentioned a moment where Dorothy seemed distracted, her gaze distant as she examined a piece of fabric. Another witness claimed to have seen her in a brief exchange with a man, though no one else corroborated this interaction.

These discrepancies raised questions about the reliability of certain witnesses. The tailor's observation of Dorothy's distraction could be attributed to the natural ebb and flow of a busy day, yet it introduced a hint of unease. The unverified account of her speaking with a man added an element of intrigue but also skepticism. Witness credibility was further scrutinized, with investigators weighing the consistency of each account against the broader narrative. Some testimonies, though detailed, lacked corroboration, while others, despite their brevity, fit seamlessly into the timeline.

The impact of these witness statements on the investigation was significant. They provided crucial leads, mapping out Dorothy's movements and interactions. Investigators followed up on these reports, visiting the shops and locations mentioned and speaking with individuals who had seen her. The bookstore clerk's detailed account led detectives to explore her interests and recent purchases, seeking clues in the literature she engaged with. The candy store employee's recollection of her cheerful mood offered a stark contrast to the darker theories of her fate. Each testimony shaped the direction of the investigation, guiding the efforts of both police and private detectives.

Conflicting accounts, however, introduced challenges. Differences in the descriptions of her behavior, even minor ones, complicated the efforts to establish a clear timeline. The tailor's report of her distraction suggested a possible internal struggle. At the same time, the uncorroborated sighting of her with a man opened the door to speculation about secret meetings or last-minute plans. These inconsistencies required careful analysis, with investigators piecing together the most plausible sequence of events. The discrepancies in timelines, though subtle, added layers of uncertainty, prompting further questioning of witnesses and re-examination of their statements.

The last confirmed sighting of Dorothy Arnold places her at the bustling intersection of Fifth Avenue and 27th Street. It was around 2:00 PM when she was seen walking alone, a solitary figure amid the throngs of shoppers and city dwellers. This precise location, a nexus of activity and commerce, was a familiar terrain for Dorothy, who frequently shopped in the area. Witnesses described her as carrying several shopping bags, indicating that she had already visited multiple stores. Her movements were purposeful, suggesting she had a clear destination in mind.

Dorothy's actions during this sighting were unremarkable on the surface. She walked with a steady pace, her posture upright, and her head held high. Those who observed her noted that she seemed composed and focused, her gaze fixed ahead as she navigated through the crowd. She did not appear to be in a hurry, nor did she seem distracted or anxious. This calm demeanor stood in stark contrast to the chaos that would follow her mysterious disappearance. She was seen adjusting one of her shopping bags, a mundane act that, in hindsight, takes on a haunting significance.

Witnesses provided detailed descriptions of Dorothy's appearance during this sighting. She wore her blue serge coat, buttoned up against the chill of the December air. Her black velvet hat, adorned with a single feather, sat elegantly on her head, casting a slight shadow over her face. The feather swayed gently with her movements, a delicate touch to her otherwise practical outfit. Her gloves were neatly fitted, and her boots clicked softly on the pavement. These details painted a vivid picture of a young woman who took pride in her appearance, even on a routine shopping trip.

Dorothy's physical state appeared normal to those who saw her. There were no signs of distress or urgency in her demeanor. Her cheeks were flushed from the cold, but her expression remained serene. She did not seem to be looking around nervously or glancing over her shoulder, behaviors that might suggest she felt threatened or uneasy. Instead, she moved with the grace and confidence of someone accustomed to the city's rhythm. Her composed exterior offered no hint of the turmoil that might have been brewing beneath the surface.

The significance of this sighting cannot be overstated. It marks the last known moment Dorothy was seen before she vanished. Fifth Avenue and 27th Street were located close to many of her planned destinations, including the shops she frequented and the potential meeting with a friend. This proximity to familiar places adds a layer of complexity to her disappearance. How could a young woman vanish so completely in an area she knew so well? The abrupt end of the trail at this busy intersection raises more questions than answers.

This particular sighting is crucial for several reasons. First, it establishes a clear timeline, pinpointing Dorothy's whereabouts at a specific time and place. This information was invaluable to investigators as they tried to reconstruct her movements and identify potential leads. Second, the sighting underscores the abruptness of her disappearance. One moment, she was walking down Fifth Avenue; the next, she was gone. In broad daylight, in a crowded area, Dorothy Arnold seemed to vanish without a trace. This sudden vanishing act defied logical explanation and fueled endless speculation.

The proximity to her planned destinations also deepens the mystery. Dorothy had mentioned shopping for a dress and possibly meeting a friend, both of which could have occurred in the vicinity of Fifth Avenue and 27th Street. The fact that she was seen carrying shopping bags suggests she had already made several purchases, aligning with her stated plans. Yet, despite these clues, no further sightings or evidence emerged to explain what happened next. The trail simply went cold, leaving her family and investigators grasping for answers.

In analyzing this sighting, one cannot help but wonder about the untapped potential for clues. Did anyone else see her after this moment? Was there something in the shopping bags that could provide insight into her plans? These questions linger, casting a shadow over the investigation. The sighting at Fifth Avenue and 27th Street remains a pivotal point in the timeline, a moment frozen in time that holds the key to understanding the mystery of Dorothy Arnold's disappearance.

THE MYSTERIOUS DISAPPEARANCE

As the evening of December 12, 1910, drew to a close, the Arnold family gathered for dinner, expecting Dorothy to return home. When she did not appear, her parents, Francis and Mary Arnold, initially believed she might have been delayed by a social engagement or perhaps shopping. However, as the hours passed and there was no word from Dorothy, concern turned to alarm. The family began to call her friends and acquaintances, hoping to find someone who had seen or heard from her that day. Each call ended the same way—no one had any information about Dorothy's whereabouts.

The first response was to keep the matter private. Ever mindful of the family's reputation, Francis Arnold decided against immediately involving the police. He feared the scandal that public knowledge of Dorothy's disappearance could ignite. Instead, he hired a private detective agency, hoping their discreet methods would yield results without attracting unwanted attention. The Pinkerton Agency, known for its expertise and discretion, was brought in to investigate. Detectives began their search, interviewing witnesses and tracing Dorothy's steps from her home to her last known location on Fifth Avenue.

Despite the family's efforts to handle the situation quietly, the lack of progress soon forced their hand. As days turned into weeks without a sign of Dorothy, the Arnolds could no longer avoid the inevitable. On January 25, 1911, more than a month after her disappearance, they filed a missing persons report with the New York City Police Department. The case quickly drew public attention, and the media frenzy began. Newspapers splashed Dorothy's photograph across their front pages, speculating wildly about her fate. The investigation now had the full force of both private detectives and the police, but still, no concrete leads emerged.

The immediate search efforts were intense and exhaustive. Family members and friends distributed flyers, canvassed neighborhoods, and followed up on any tips they received. Private detectives scoured the city, visiting hospitals and morgues, checking for any unidentified women matching Dorothy's description. The police conducted their own search, questioning anyone who might have seen or spoken to her that day. Despite these efforts, no substantial clues were found. Dorothy seemed to have vanished into thin air, leaving no trace of what had happened to her.

Theories abounded in the weeks following Dorothy's disappearance. Each one a story unto itself, casting new shadows and uncovering fresh mysteries. From a carefully planned escape to a darker end, these theories added both intrigue and confusion.

Theories about Dorothy's disappearance began to circulate, each more sensational than the last. One possible scenario was abduction. Given her family's wealth and social standing, some speculated that Dorothy might have been kidnapped for ransom. However, no ransom demands were ever made, and no evidence supported this theory. Another theory was that she had voluntarily disappeared, seeking to escape the pressures of her social life. Dorothy's desire for independence and her frustrations with societal expectations lent some credence to this idea. Yet, there was no indication that she had prepared for such a drastic step.

The lack of concrete evidence further fueled the mystery. How could a young woman disappear so entirely in broad daylight in one of the busiest cities in the world? The unanswered questions were numerous and perplexing. How did she vanish without leaving any trace? Why was there no physical evidence, no sightings, no credible leads? The absence of any concrete clues only deepened the enigma, leaving both investigators and the public grasping for answers.

As the days turned into months, hope began to wane. The Arnold family was left to grapple with their grief and the endless speculation. Dorothy's fate remained an open question, a haunting void that defied resolution. The theories, the searches, the witness accounts—all led to dead ends. The mystery of her disappearance became a symbol of the era's limitations in investigative techniques and the societal pressures that shaped her life.

This chapter closes with the stark reality that despite all efforts, Dorothy Arnold's disappearance remains one of the most baffling, unsolved cases of the early 20th century. The lack of evidence and the unanswered questions cast a long shadow over the investigation, leaving a legacy of intrigue and sadness. The mystery of what happened to Dorothy Arnold continues to captivate and confound, inviting endless speculation and reflection on the societal dynamics of her time. This abrupt end of Dorothy's trail sets the stage for deeper exploration into the broader implications of her disappearance and the societal factors at play. The next chapter will delve into the intricate web of family dynamics, media involvement, and the lasting impact of her mysterious vanishing.

CHAPTER 3

THE INITIAL INVESTIGATION

The Arnold family's emotional struggles are brought to life by highlighting tensions between Francis, Mary, and Elsie as they cope with Dorothy's disappearance. Personal anecdotes, speculative letters, and potential family dialogues offer an intimate perspective, humanizing the family and portraying the profound impact of the investigation on their lives. This chapter explores the societal implications of their choice to keep the disappearance private, showing how high society often prioritized reputation over transparency.

THE ARNOLD FAMILY'S FIRST REACTIONS

As dusk settled over New York City on December 12, 1910, the Arnold family began to realize that something was terribly wrong. Dorothy had not returned home, and the hours stretched into an uneasy night. The grand home on the Upper East Side, usually a beacon of order and routine, was now a place of growing anxiety. Francis Arnold, Dorothy's father, paced the floor of the parlor, his formidable presence now tinged with worry. He was a man used to control, known for his strict discipline both in business and at home. But tonight, his authority felt powerless against the unknown.

The family convened an impromptu meeting, gathering around the dining room table that had seen its share of both celebrations and conflicts. The atmosphere was heavy, each member grappling with their own fears. Francis, his face drawn and serious, led the discussion. He proposed they start by calling Dorothy's friends and acquaintances, hoping someone had seen her or heard from her. Mary Arnold, Dorothy's mother, clutched a handkerchief, her eyes wide with disbelief. She had always been the emotional anchor of the family, but now she found herself adrift in a sea of uncertainty, barely holding on to her composure.

The initial phone calls were a mix of hope and dread. Francis dialed each number with a steady hand, his voice calm but urgent. He spoke with Dorothy's closest friends, her college acquaintances, and even casual social contacts. Each conversation ended the same way—no one had seen Dorothy since that afternoon. The lack of information only heightened the family's anxiety. Mary sat beside the phone, her fingers twisting the handkerchief into knots, her mind racing through worst-case scenarios. She could not reconcile the image of her vibrant, capable daughter with the possibility that she was in danger.

Elsie Arnold, Dorothy's younger sister, watched the proceedings with a mix of fear and determination. She idolized Dorothy, who had always been her confidante and role model. Elsie's mind churned with questions. Where could Dorothy be? Why hadn't she come home? She felt a gnawing guilt, wondering if she had missed any signs of distress or plans Dorothy might have made. Elsie offered to contact some of Dorothy's more distant friends, hoping a broader search might yield some clues. Her actions were driven by a desperate need to contribute, to do something, anything, to find her sister.

As the night wore on, the family faced a critical decision: whether to keep Dorothy's disappearance private or to seek broader help. Francis argued for discretion. He was acutely aware of the societal implications of making the news public. The Arnold family's reputation was built on a foundation of respectability and control. Any hint of scandal could shatter that facade. Francis feared the gossip and speculation that would inevitably follow. He believed that handling the matter internally, at least initially, would protect the family from public scrutiny.

Mary, however, was less convinced. Her maternal instincts screamed for action, for any step that might bring Dorothy back. She worried that delaying a public search would only reduce their chances of finding her. Yet, she also understood Francis's concerns. The delicate balance of their social standing was not something to be taken lightly. In the end, Francis's argument won out. The family decided to quietly hire private detectives, hoping their professional expertise would yield results without attracting unwanted attention.

The decision to keep the disappearance private created an undercurrent of tension within the family. Mary struggled with the feeling that they were not doing enough, her worry manifesting in sleepless nights and constant agitation. Her maternal instinct warred with the constraints of propriety, leaving her caught in an internal struggle that deepened as each day passed. Francis, though outwardly composed, felt the strain of maintaining a facade of control. His frustration grew with each day that passed without news. He threw himself into his work, using it as a distraction from the gnawing fear that something terrible had happened to his daughter. Elsie, meanwhile, found herself caught between her parents' conflicting approaches. She supported her father's decision but shared her mother's anxiety and sense of helplessness.

The internal dynamics of the Arnold family shifted under the weight of the crisis. Conflicts and disagreements became more frequent. Mary and Francis argued over the best course of action, their discussions sometimes devolving into heated exchanges. Francis, normally so rational, began snapping more frequently, while Mary grew increasingly emotional, each blaming the other for perceived inaction. Elsie found herself playing the role of mediator, trying to maintain a semblance of harmony. The normally composed household was now a place of emotional volatility. The stress took its toll on everyone, eroding the usual support structures and leaving each family member feeling isolated in their own way.

Despite the tensions, there were also moments of solidarity. The family rallied around the shared goal of finding Dorothy, their love for her a unifying force. They made concerted efforts to maintain composure and normalcy, both for their own sake and to avoid arousing suspicion among their social circle. Publicly, they continued to attend social events and fulfill their obligations, presenting a united front. Privately, their world was falling apart, each day without news, deepening the chasm of fear and uncertainty.

As you walk through these moments with the Arnold family, you can feel the weight of their decisions and the emotional toll it took on them. Their immediate response to Dorothy's disappearance was a blend of practical action and profound emotional turmoil. The tension between the need to protect their reputation and the desperate desire to find their daughter created a complex web of choices and consequences. The family's initial reactions set the stage for the broader investigation that would follow, a journey marked by hope, frustration, and an unyielding quest for answers.

HIRING PRIVATE INVESTIGATORS: THE PINKERTON AGENCY

When the Arnold family decided to seek outside help, they turned to the Pinkerton National Detective Agency. Known for their expertise and discretion, the Pinkertons were a logical choice for a family deeply concerned about their public image. The agency's reputation was built on solving high-profile cases, and their motto, "We Never Sleep," symbolized their relentless pursuit of justice. Ever the pragmatic businessman Francis Arnold believed that the Pinkertons' resources and methods would yield answers without the unwanted glare of media attention.

The initial meeting between the Arnold family and the Pinkertons was a somber affair. Francis Arnold, accompanied by a trusted family lawyer, laid out the facts of Dorothy's disappearance with a precision that spoke to his desperation. The Pinkerton representatives listened intently, their expressions grave as they took notes. The contract details were swiftly handled, with the family agreeing to a significant retainer fee in exchange for the agency's full commitment to the case. The Pinkertons assured them that every possible lead would be pursued, every stone turned, in the search for Dorothy.

The Pinkerton Agency wasted no time in deploying their seasoned detectives. Their investigative methods were comprehensive and multifaceted. Surveillance and stakeouts became a staple of their efforts. Operatives were assigned to monitor key locations, such as the Arnold residence and the shops Dorothy had visited on the day of her disappearance. These stakeouts were meticulous, with agents working in shifts to ensure constant vigilance. They watched for any suspicious activity, hoping to catch a glimpse of Dorothy or uncover a clue that could lead them to her.

Interviews with potential witnesses formed another crucial part of the Pinkerton strategy. Detectives revisited every shop Dorothy had entered, speaking with clerks and customers alike. They combed through witness testimonies, cross-referencing details to build a coherent timeline of her last known movements. The agency's operatives were skilled in eliciting information, using both charm and persistence to extract even the smallest details. They also expanded their search to include anyone who might have seen Dorothy in the days leading up to her disappearance, broadening the scope of their investigation.

Undercover operatives played a pivotal role in the Pinkerton investigation. These agents, often disguised as ordinary citizens, infiltrated social circles and environments where they might glean information about Dorothy's fate. They attended social gatherings, frequented popular haunts, and engaged in casual conversations, all the while keeping their true purpose hidden. The aim was to gather intelligence without raising suspicion and to blend in seamlessly while observing and listening. These undercover efforts were particularly focused on areas where rumors and gossip about Dorothy's disappearance might circulate.

Despite their thorough methods, the Pinkertons faced significant challenges. Leads were generated and pursued, but many ended in dead ends. The initial flurry of activity yielded a few promising hints but none that brought them closer to finding Dorothy. The lack of concrete evidence was a constant frustration. Each day that passed without new information felt like a setback, a reminder of the elusive nature of the case. The detectives remained undeterred, but the limitations of their efforts became increasingly apparent.

The collaboration between the Pinkertons and the police was both a boon and a source of tension. While both parties shared the common goal of finding Dorothy, their methods and priorities sometimes clashed. The Pinkertons, bound by their contract to maintain discretion, were cautious about sharing information with law enforcement. The police, on the other hand, were keen to leverage the agency's resources but chafed at the restrictions. Information and resources were exchanged, but the coordination was often fraught with misunderstandings and disagreements.

Points of contention included the handling of witness testimonies and the prioritization of leads. The Pinkertons, with their focus on discretion, sometimes held back details that the police deemed crucial. Conversely, the police's need for transparency and public accountability occasionally conflicted with the agency's methods. Despite these challenges, there were moments of cooperation that proved fruitful. Joint efforts in canvassing neighborhoods and following up on public tips demonstrated the potential for collaboration, even amid differing approaches.

In the shadow of these efforts, the Arnold family watched and waited. Each report from the Pinkertons brought a mix of hope and despair, a reminder of the relentless uncertainty that defined their days. The private investigators' work was a double-edged sword—offering both the promise of resolution and the stark reality of the obstacles they faced. The search for Dorothy Arnold was a labyrinthine endeavor marked by methodical investigation and the ever-present specter of the unknown.

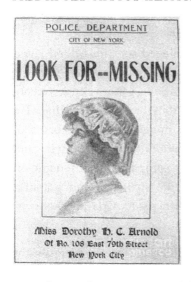

POLICE DEPARTMENT
CITY OF NEW YORK

LOOK FOR--MISSING

Miss Dorothy H. C. Arnold
Of No. 108 East 79th Street
New York City

The story of Dorothy Arnold's disappearance broke in the press with a fervor that matched New York's unrelenting energy. The first headlines appeared almost six weeks after she vanished, with newspapers like The New York Times and the New York Herald leading the charge. "Heiress Disappears Without a Trace!" and "Mystery of the Missing Socialite" screamed from the front pages, capturing the public's imagination. The initial articles provided scant details but were laden with speculation, hinting at scandal and intrigue. The public's curiosity was piqued, and the story quickly became the talk of the town.

The role of yellow journalism, in this case, cannot be overstated. Newspapers, eager to boost sales, engaged in sensationalized reporting that often blurred the lines between fact and fiction. Exaggerated headlines and lurid stories became the norm. One paper suggested a secret lover, another hinted at a botched abortion. These narratives, often unsupported by evidence, shaped public perception in profound ways. The Arnold family's privacy was invaded, and their every move was scrutinized and reported. The relentless media coverage turned their personal tragedy into a public spectacle, adding to their anguish and complicating their search for Dorothy.

Dorothy's social status as a wealthy heiress significantly influenced the media coverage. Reporters focused on her position in high society, emphasizing her luxurious lifestyle and familial connections. Articles detailed the Arnold family's lineage, tracing their roots back to the Mayflower, and highlighted their opulent Upper East Side residence. Dorothy's fashion choices, her education at Bryn Mawr College, and her failed attempts to become a writer were all fodder for public consumption. Speculative stories about her personal life, including her secret relationship with George Griscom Jr., an unemployed bachelor deemed unsuitable by her father, filled the pages of countless newspapers.

The media's portrayal of Dorothy as a privileged socialite added layers of complexity to the narrative. While some articles painted her as a tragic figure constrained by societal expectations, others suggested she might have used her wealth and connections to escape her life. The public was fascinated by these conflicting images, and the story took on a life of its own. The wealth and status of the Arnold family became a double-edged sword, attracting both sympathy and suspicion. Speculative stories about Dorothy's personal struggles and potential secrets fueled endless gossip, making it difficult to separate fact from fiction.

The influence of press coverage on the investigation was significant. Articles generated public tips and leads, some credible, others wildly speculative. The media frenzy prompted a flood of information, overwhelming both the Pinkerton detectives and the police. Well-meaning citizens reported sightings of Dorothy from as far away as California and Europe, though none could be verified. Law enforcement and private investigators faced pressure to follow up on every lead, no matter how tenuous. This deluge of information, while initially promising, often led to dead ends and false hopes.

The relentless media attention also placed immense pressure on the Arnold family and the investigators. The public's demand for answers and the sensationalized narratives created a high-stakes environment. Detectives were compelled to work under the scrutiny of the press, their every move analyzed and critiqued. This scrutiny sometimes led to hasty decisions and missteps, further complicating the investigation. The need to provide updates and maintain public interest often overshadowed the meticulous, methodical work required to uncover the truth.

As the story of Dorothy Arnold's disappearance continued to captivate the public, the media's role evolved. Initial curiosity turned into sustained interest, with newspapers running regular updates and new theories. The Arnold family, initially reluctant to engage with the press, found themselves drawn into the narrative, issuing statements and holding press conferences in a bid to control the story. Despite their efforts, the media machine churned on, each new headline adding another layer to the mystery.

The case of Dorothy Arnold illustrates the powerful influence of the media in shaping public perception and influencing investigations. The sensationalized reporting, the focus on her social status, and the relentless scrutiny created an environment where truth and speculation became intertwined. The media's role in this case is a testament to the complex interplay between public interest, journalistic ambition, and the search for answers in a world captivated by the unknown.

THE POLICE INVOLVEMENT: EARLY EFFORTS AND CHALLENGES

When the Arnold family finally turned to the police, the formal reporting process began with a sense of urgency. Francis Arnold, accompanied by a family lawyer, visited the precinct to file a missing person report. The police, already aware of the media buzz surrounding Dorothy's disappearance, immediately recognized the gravity of the situation. Detectives were promptly assigned to the case, with the lead investigator, Captain John Ayers, taking charge. His reputation for solving complex cases made him a fitting choice, but even he knew this would be no ordinary investigation.

The early stages of the investigation were fraught with challenges. The lack of concrete evidence was a significant hurdle. Dorothy had vanished without leaving any physical traces—no signs of a struggle, no witnesses who saw anything suspicious. The detectives found themselves working with a blank slate. Compounding this issue was the limited cooperation from the Arnold family. Francis's initial decision to keep the disappearance private meant the crucial time had already been lost. The family, still wary of public scandal, was cautious in their interactions with law enforcement. This hesitance created a barrier, making it difficult for detectives to gather comprehensive background information on Dorothy.

The police employed several methods and strategies to tackle the case. Canvassing the neighborhood was one of the first steps. Officers went door to door, speaking with residents and shopkeepers in the area where Dorothy was last seen. They hoped to uncover any overlooked details or witness statements that might provide new leads. The detectives also followed up on numerous tips from the public, most of which led to dead ends. Each tip, no matter how trivial, was meticulously logged and pursued. The detectives knew that even the smallest detail could potentially break the case wide open.

Despite their best efforts, the police investigation faced significant obstacles. The media scrutiny added a layer of complexity. Reporters hounded the precinct for updates, often sensationalizing minor details and creating a circus-like atmosphere. The pressure to provide answers quickly was immense. This environment made it difficult for detectives to conduct their work methodically. The need to balance public expectations with the realities of investigative work became a daily struggle.

The effectiveness of the police investigation was a mixed bag. Some leads were promising, but many fizzled out. The canvassing efforts yielded a few new witness statements but none that brought them closer to finding Dorothy. The detectives' persistence in following up on public tips demonstrated their commitment, yet the sheer volume of false leads drained resources and morale. The collaboration with the Pinkerton Agency also had its ups and downs. While the shared goal was clear, differences in approach and priorities sometimes led to friction.

One notable success was the identification of Dorothy's last known movements through witness testimonies and shop records. This helped establish a clearer timeline, which was crucial for piecing together her final hours. However, the lack of physical evidence continued to be a stumbling block. Without tangible clues, the investigation was like chasing shadows. The detectives found themselves revisiting the same questions, hoping for a breakthrough that remained elusive.

As days turned into weeks, the sense of urgency grew. The police, despite their best efforts, were no closer to solving the mystery. The frustration within the precinct was palpable. Detectives worked long hours, driven by a mix of professional duty and personal investment in the case. They knew the eyes of the city were upon them, and the pressure to deliver answers was relentless. Yet, the more they dug, the more the mystery deepened.

The impact of media scrutiny on police work was profound. The constant barrage of headlines and public interest created an environment where every action was magnified. Detailing even minor developments to the press became a delicate balancing act. The detectives had to navigate the fine line between maintaining public trust and protecting the integrity of the investigation. This scrutiny often led to second-guessing and re-evaluating strategies, further complicating an already complex case.

In the end, the police's early efforts were marked by a combination of dedication and frustration. The initial involvement of law enforcement brought structure and resources to the search for Dorothy, but the challenges they faced underscored the difficulties of solving such an enigmatic case. The detectives' commitment to finding answers, despite the obstacles, highlighted the relentless pursuit of justice that defined the investigation.

THE ROLE OF SOCIAL STANDING IN THE INVESTIGATION

Dorothy Arnold's disappearance was not just another missing person case; it was a high-profile mystery involving one of New York's most prominent families. The Arnold family's social standing played a crucial role in shaping the investigation, offering both advantages and disadvantages. On one hand, their wealth and influence provided unparalleled access to resources. The family could afford to hire the best private investigators, including the renowned Pinkerton Agency. They leveraged their influential contacts, calling on favors from friends in high places to expedite the search. This network included business associates, politicians, and even members of the media, all of whom could potentially offer leads or push the investigation forward.

However, this high social status also brought significant public and media scrutiny. The Arnold family's prominence made Dorothy's disappearance a sensational story, capturing the attention of newspapers and the public alike. Every move the family made was dissected, every decision second-guessed. This relentless scrutiny added a layer of complexity to an already challenging situation. The media's intense focus on the case meant that any misstep could become front-page news, further complicating efforts to find Dorothy. The family's attempts to maintain privacy only fueled speculation, with the press eager to uncover any hidden secrets or scandals.

Public perception of the Arnold family was a mixed bag of sympathy and suspicion. Many people felt genuine empathy for the family, understanding the anguish they must be experiencing. Dorothy's social status and the picturesque life she led made her a relatable figure to many, evoking a sense of shared humanity. Yet, there was also a darker side to public opinion. Some saw the family's wealth and influence as a shield, protecting them from the full force of the law. Rumors and whispers suggested that the Arnolds might be hiding something, that their reluctance to cooperate with the police fully was a sign of guilt or complicity. This duality in public perception created an atmosphere of intrigue and uncertainty, further muddying the waters of the investigation.

The impact of social class on investigative priorities was evident. The Arnold family's status ensured that Dorothy's case received immediate and sustained attention from law enforcement. Unlike many other missing person cases of the time, which often languished in obscurity, Dorothy's disappearance was a high-priority matter. Resources were allocated generously, with both the police and private investigators working tirelessly to uncover the truth. This level of attention was a direct result of the family's social standing, highlighting the disparities in how cases were handled based on the victim's background.

Comparing Dorothy's case to other missing person cases of the era reveals stark differences. Many disappearances involving individuals from lower socioeconomic backgrounds received minimal attention, their investigations hampered by a lack of resources and public interest. In contrast, Dorothy's case was propelled into the spotlight, her family's influence ensuring that no stone was left unturned. This disparity underscores the broader societal issues of the time, where wealth and status often dictated the level of justice one could expect.

The societal implications of Dorothy Arnold's disappearance go beyond the immediate investigation. The case highlighted the deep class divisions within early 20th-century New York and the different ways justice was perceived and administered. The media portrayal of Dorothy and her family, juxtaposed against the treatment of ordinary citizens, offered a stark commentary on social inequality. The relentless focus on her socialite status, her luxurious lifestyle, and the family's influential connections painted a picture of a world where privilege was both a blessing and a curse.

Class divisions were further accentuated by the public's reaction to the case. The fascination with Dorothy's disappearance was partly driven by her status as a socialite, a figure who embodied both the allure and the constraints of high society. The public's insatiable curiosity about her life and fate was a reflection of broader societal dynamics, where the lives of the wealthy were both envied and scrutinized. The case also raised questions about the nature of justice and fairness, prompting reflections on how societal structures influenced the pursuit of truth.

As the investigation unfolded, it became clear that Dorothy Arnold's disappearance was not just a family tragedy but a societal event. The case exposed the intricate interplay between wealth, influence, and justice, offering a lens through which the complexities of early 20th-century New York could be examined. The role of social standing in shaping the investigation and public perception was a key element, highlighting the broader implications of Dorothy's mysterious vanishing.

The next chapter will delve deeper into the theories surrounding Dorothy's disappearance, exploring the various possibilities and the evidence that supports or refutes them. From a botched abortion to a planned escape, the theories are as varied as they are compelling, each adding another layer to the enigma that continues to captivate and confound.

CHAPTER 4

MEDIA FRENZY AND PUBLIC SPECULATION

The role of the press was twofold: while it brought widespread attention to Dorothy's case, it also sensationalized her life and the investigation. Newspapers operated with a fierce competition for readership, often exaggerating details or fabricating theories for the sake of captivating their audience. This had a direct impact on the family, placing them under an intense public microscope and complicating their search efforts as police were forced to follow up on false leads fueled by journalistic speculation.

YELLOW JOURNALISM: SENSATIONALIZED REPORTING

Dorothy Arnold's disappearance gripped New York City like a fever. The story of the missing heiress was a goldmine for newspapers, and they wasted no time capitalizing on it. Headlines like "Vanished Heiress Baffles Police" dominated the front pages, turning Dorothy's case into a public spectacle. The press, driven by competition and the public's insatiable appetite for scandal, dove headfirst into yellow journalism. This style of reporting, characterized by its sensationalism and lack of factual grounding, turned speculative stories into front-page news, overshadowing any factual leads and distorting the investigation.

The rise of yellow journalism in the early 1900s marked a turning point in how the media covered high-profile cases. In a fierce competition for readership, newspapers like William Randolph Hearst's New York Journal prioritized scandal over truth. The ethical lines were blurred, and facts became secondary to selling stories. Headlines were designed to evoke shock, fear, and curiosity. This environment laid the groundwork for an era where the media's portrayal of cases like Dorothy's would have far-reaching consequences on both public perception and investigative efforts.

Newspapers employed a range of sensational tactics to draw readers into Dorothy's disappearance. The use of exaggerated and misleading headlines was the first line of attack. Bold, dramatic titles screamed from newsstands, promising shocking revelations. "Heiress Abducted by Secret Lover?" and "Did Dorothy Arnold Commit Suicide?" were the kind of headlines that sold papers, regardless of their veracity. These titles were carefully crafted to evoke strong emotions and curiosity, ensuring the public stayed hooked. Other tactics included the use of dramatic and emotional language in articles, and the publication of unverified rumors as though they were facts.

Amid this frenzy, the psychological toll on the Arnold family became ever more apparent. Every morning, as the family gathered for breakfast, the sound of the newspaper hitting their doorstep was a stark reminder that their private tragedy had become public property. Francis, once the epitome of control, felt his grip on his family's narrative slipping away. He would skim the headlines, feeling a mixture of rage and helplessness. Mary, usually so composed, found herself crying quietly over her coffee, unable to bear reading the lurid speculations about her daughter. Each article felt like another blow, exacerbating their grief and anxiety. The invasion of their privacy was relentless, and the family's distress was palpable.

Another hallmark of yellow journalism was the use of dramatic and emotional language. Articles were written to provoke a visceral response, using words designed to incite fear, sympathy, or outrage. Descriptions of Dorothy's beauty and social standing were interwoven with dark, speculative narratives, painting a picture of a tragic figure caught in a web of mystery and intrigue. This use of language transformed the story from a simple missing person case into a melodrama that captivated the public's imagination. The emotional manipulation in the language used was evident, and it played a significant role in distorting the public's perception of the case.

Unverified rumors were published as though they were facts. Newspapers didn't hesitate to report on hearsay or speculation, often without any corroborating evidence. Stories about secret lovers, botched abortions, and even foul play became common, each one adding a new layer to the already tangled narrative. These rumors spread like wildfire, each one more sensational than the last, feeding the public's appetite for scandal and deepening the mystery surrounding Dorothy's fate. The lack of factual grounding not only misled the public but also derailed the investigation, as police and private detectives found themselves chasing leads generated by these fabricated stories.

Prominent publications and journalists played pivotal roles in this media frenzy. The New York Times, known for its influence and reach, covered the case extensively, often walking the line between factual reporting and sensationalism. William Randolph Hearst's newspapers, including the New York Journal, were at the forefront of yellow journalism. Hearst, a powerful media mogul known for his sensationalist approach, used his papers to push the most dramatic and lurid angles of the story. Influential journalists of the time, like Arthur Brisbane, one of Hearst's star editors, penned articles that captured the public's attention with their vivid storytelling and speculative content.

The emotional strain this constant media coverage placed on the Arnold family was immeasurable. Francis found his business and personal life entangled in a web of public scrutiny, something he had spent his entire life trying to avoid. Mary, once a private and composed figure, was now forced into the public eye, her grief magnified under the unforgiving gaze of the press. Every glance, every word spoken in public, was dissected, reported, and misinterpreted by eager journalists. Elsie, too, could not escape the relentless speculation, often seeing her name linked to unverified rumors about Dorothy's disappearance.

The impact of this sensationalism on public perception was profound. The exaggerated reporting created an atmosphere of panic and intrigue. The public, already captivated by the idea of a missing heiress, found themselves drawn deeper into the narrative with each new headline. Misinformation spread rapidly as people took the sensational stories at face value. The line between fact and fiction is blurred, making it difficult for the public to discern the truth. This widespread misinformation not only fueled public curiosity but also complicated the investigation, as tips and leads based on false narratives flooded in, diverting resources and attention from more credible avenues. The impact of sensationalism on public perception was significant, and it raised concerns about the public's ability to distinguish between fact and fiction.

The ethical implications of yellow journalism in Dorothy Arnold's case are significant. The lack of fact-checking and verification in reporting led to a proliferation of false information. Journalists, driven by the pressure to sell newspapers, prioritized sensationalism over accuracy. This approach compromised the integrity of the news and had real consequences for the investigation and the Arnold family. The pressure to constantly produce dramatic stories often led to the publication of unverified rumors, which then shaped public opinion and influenced the course of the investigation.

Reflecting on the journalistic standards of the time, it's clear that the pursuit of sensationalism often overshadowed the responsibility to report the truth. The ethical lapses in reporting not only distorted the investigation but also had a lasting impact on the public's trust in the media. The case of Dorothy Arnold serves as a poignant example of the dangers of yellow journalism and the far-reaching effects of sensationalized reporting. The press's relentless focus on scandal and intrigue turned a tragic disappearance into a public spectacle, complicating the search for truth and justice.

PUBLIC REACTIONS AND SPECULATIONS

The public's reaction to Dorothy Arnold's disappearance was not just immediate but also deeply emotional. The news of the missing heiress spread like wildfire, sparking a wave of shock, curiosity, and concern. People from all walks of life found themselves captivated by the mystery. Discussions about Dorothy's fate became a common topic at dinner tables, in cafés, and on street corners. The collective anxiety and fascination led to the formation of amateur search parties composed of concerned citizens eager to help. These groups scoured parks, alleys, and abandoned buildings, driven by the hope of finding any trace of Dorothy.

As the media circus unfolded, the public's emotional investment in the case deepened. Theories began to take on lives of their own, circulating through the city like whispered secrets. It wasn't just the newspapers feeding speculation—word-of-mouth spread through the streets as amateur detectives began to form their own opinions. The public's imagination ran wild, fueled by the media's constant stream of exaggerated reporting. Sensational theories about Dorothy's fate became the subject of debate, with some convinced she had been abducted, while others believed she had eloped with a secret lover. Each new theory only heightened the tension and intrigue, ensuring that the case would remain at the forefront of public consciousness for weeks on end.

Speculations about what might have happened to Dorothy began to swirl almost as soon as the news broke. One of the most popular theories was that she had eloped with a secret lover. The idea of a young socialite running away for love captured the public's imagination. Others speculated about foul play, suggesting that Dorothy had been abducted or met with violence. The notion of a wealthy heiress being targeted for her fortune seemed plausible to many. Equally compelling was the theory that Dorothy had met with an accident, possibly during a botched abortion. This dark speculation fed into the era's anxieties about women's autonomy and the risks associated with seeking independence.

The idea that Dorothy might have voluntarily disappeared also held sway. Many were fascinated by the possibility that she had chosen to escape the pressures of her life. The notion of a socialite abandoning her privileged existence for anonymity was both shocking and alluring. It spoke to the societal pressures faced by women of her status and the lengths they might go to for freedom. Each theory, despite the lack of concrete evidence, found its adherents, reflecting the diverse anxieties and hopes of the public.

Public figures and opinion leaders played significant roles in shaping the discourse around Dorothy's disappearance. Politicians and celebrities weighed in, their statements adding gravity to the ongoing speculation. Some used their platforms to express sympathy for the Arnold family, urging the public to respect their privacy. Others, however, fueled the rumors, making bold claims about what might have happened. Community leaders also contributed to the conversation, often reflecting the sentiments of their constituencies. Their influence helped to shape the narrative, guiding public opinion in subtle yet powerful ways.

The reactions from different social groups added layers to the public speculation. High-society families, familiar with the pressures of maintaining a public image, often expressed a mix of sympathy and concern. They understood the stakes and the scrutiny that came with such a high-profile case. The working-class community, on the other hand, viewed the situation through a different lens. For them, the idea of a wealthy socialite disappearing was both a source of intrigue and a reminder of the stark divides in society. Their speculations were often tinged with skepticism, questioning whether the Arnold family's influence might be obscuring the truth.

As the weeks passed, amateur sleuths and armchair detectives emerged, each offering their own interpretations of the scant evidence available. These individuals, driven by curiosity and a desire to solve the mystery, pored over newspaper articles and followed every new development closely. They formed theories based on their own experiences and biases, adding to the cacophony of voices surrounding the case. Despite their enthusiasm, none of these theories could be confirmed, leaving the mystery as impenetrable as ever.

The societal dynamics at play were complex. Dorothy's disappearance highlighted the tensions between wealth and power and the public's fascination with high-society scandals. It also reflected deeper anxieties about women's roles and autonomy. Each theory, whether about elopement, abduction, or voluntary disappearance, spoke to the fears and fantasies of the time. The public's engagement with the case was not just about finding answers; it was about grappling with the broader societal issues that Dorothy's disappearance had brought to the fore.

In the midst of this public speculation, the Arnold family found themselves caught in a whirlwind of rumors and theories. The investigation continued, but the cacophony of public opinion made it increasingly difficult to discern fact from fiction. The myriad speculations, though often baseless, painted a vivid picture of a society grappling with its own anxieties and curiosities, reflecting the complex interplay between public perception and personal tragedy.

MEDIA INFLUENCE ON THE ARNOLD FAMILY

The media's relentless focus on Dorothy's disappearance put an unbearable strain on the Arnold family. Their lives once lived in the privacy afforded by wealth and status, were now subject to the scrutiny of the public. The constant barrage of headlines, speculation, and false leads transformed their home into a fortress. Photographers and reporters camped outside their mansion on the Upper East Side, hoping to capture any sign of the grieving family. Every time the curtains were drawn, or a car left the driveway, it was reported in minute detail, feeding the public's hunger for any sliver of information.

Francis Arnold, a man who had always maintained control, found his carefully crafted life falling apart. His interactions with the press became increasingly fraught with tension as he struggled to navigate the delicate balance between maintaining his family's privacy and providing enough information to quell public curiosity. Behind closed doors, the strain was even greater. He was frustrated, not only by the lack of progress in the investigation but by the feeling that he could not protect his family from the media's intrusion.

Mary Arnold, too, found herself in the crosshairs of public attention. As a mother, she felt every article, every headline, as an attack on her family. The press, with their insatiable appetite for scandal, had no regard for her grief. They painted her as either a heartbroken mother or an aloof matriarch, depending on the day. The constant scrutiny deepened her sense of helplessness. No matter how hard she tried to shield her family, the media's relentless coverage seeped into every aspect of their lives.

Elsie Arnold, Dorothy's younger sister, had a unique burden to bear. She was thrust into the spotlight, her every move and word analyzed by the press. Speculation about her relationship with Dorothy became a topic of public conversation. Was there sibling rivalry? Had she known something about Dorothy's disappearance? These rumors were particularly painful for Elsie as they compounded her already overwhelming grief. The media's relentless focus on her family's tragedy left her feeling exposed and vulnerable.

In response to the media onslaught, the Arnolds attempted to take control of the narrative. They held press conferences, issued statements, and hired public relations experts to manage their interactions with the press. Despite these efforts, they struggled to contain the flood of rumors and misinformation. At times, it felt as if the harder they tried to maintain their dignity, the more the press sought to tear them down. Legal actions were taken against publications that crossed the line, but even lawsuits did little to stem the tide of sensational reporting.

One of the most significant media interactions was an interview with Francis Arnold, in which he vehemently denied rumors of a family rift or financial troubles. His frustration was palpable as he tried to dispel the growing number of baseless theories that had come to dominate the media coverage. It was a rare glimpse into the emotional toll the disappearance was taking on the family, though even this moment of vulnerability was quickly spun by the press to suit their own narratives.

The psychological and emotional toll of this constant media scrutiny was profound. The Arnold family, already grappling with the disappearance of their daughter, now found themselves navigating a secondary crisis: managing their public image in the face of relentless gossip and scandal. Their private grief had been turned into a public spectacle, and there was no escaping the invasive gaze of the press.

Over time, the family became more guarded. The once open and sociable Arnolds retreated into themselves, wary of any interaction that might be misinterpreted or exploited by the media. The wounds inflicted by this constant scrutiny were deep and long-lasting, changing the way the family interacted with the world. The public's hunger for scandal had complicated the search for Dorothy, adding layers of stress and anxiety to an already unbearable situation.

THE SOCIETAL VIEWS ON WOMEN AND CRIME

In the early 1900s, societal expectations for women were stringent and unyielding. Dorothy Arnold, as a wealthy woman, was expected to marry well and contribute to her family's status through charitable work and social engagements. These roles were not merely suggestions; they were mandates that governed every aspect of a woman's life. Women were seen as the keepers of virtue and domestic harmony, their actions closely monitored to ensure they upheld the family's honor. Dorothy's aspiration to become a writer was a bold defiance of these norms. Her family did not support her ambitions, viewing them as frivolous pursuits that could tarnish their reputation. Her disappearance became more than a personal tragedy; it was a cautionary tale for other young women who dared to seek independence in a society that stifled them.

The prevailing attitudes of 1910 viewed women through a lens of fragility and dependence. Men were the protectors and providers, while women were expected to embody purity and domesticity. Female independence was often met with suspicion and disapproval. Women who stepped outside their prescribed roles were considered rebellious and were often ostracized. This cultural backdrop influenced how Dorothy's disappearance was perceived. The public and investigators alike were quick to speculate that her disappearance might be linked to her defiance of societal norms. The idea that a woman of her standing could vanish was unfathomable, leading many to believe that her pursuit of independence had led her into dangerous territory.

The media's portrayal of women during this era was deeply influenced by these societal norms. Newspapers often depicted Dorothy and other women as delicate and vulnerable, emphasizing their femininity and need for protection. Articles about Dorothy highlighted her beauty, her social status, and her supposed naiveté. These descriptions served to reinforce the idea that women were inherently vulnerable and in need of male guardianship. In contrast, male figures in similar situations were portrayed as strong and capable, their disappearances framed as adventures or heroic undertakings. This gendered portrayal in the media not only shaped public perception but also influenced the direction of the investigation.

Investigative priorities and methods were heavily influenced by these gender biases. Assumptions about women's behavior and choices often led to dismissive attitudes towards certain theories. For instance, the idea that Dorothy might have run away voluntarily was initially met with skepticism. Investigators found it hard to believe that a young woman of her status would choose to abandon her privileged life. This bias impacted the credibility of various leads, causing some potential avenues of investigation to be neglected. The focus often remained on more sensational theories, such as abduction or foul play, which aligned more closely with societal views of women's vulnerability.

Dorothy Arnold's case reflects broader cultural implications regarding women and crime. Her disappearance highlighted the limitations placed on women and the societal pressures they faced. It brought to light the double standards in how male and female victims were perceived and treated. The case also underscored the need for changes in public and legal attitudes towards women. Over time, Dorothy's story contributed to a growing awareness of the issues surrounding women's autonomy and the biases inherent in the criminal justice system. It served as a catalyst for discussions about gender equality and the importance of supporting women's independence.

The long-term changes in public and legal attitudes towards women can be traced back to cases like Dorothy's. Her disappearance and the media frenzy that followed exposed the flaws in how women were viewed and treated by society. It prompted a reevaluation of the roles and expectations placed on women, leading to gradual shifts in societal norms. Future cases involving women began to be approached with a greater understanding of the complexities surrounding female independence and victimhood. The legacy of Dorothy Arnold's case is a testament to the enduring impact of societal views on women and crime and the slow but inevitable progress towards gender equality.

THE ROLE OF GOSSIP AND SCANDAL

The disappearance of Dorothy Arnold became more than a news story; it turned into a social phenomenon fueled by the relentless spread of gossip and rumors. In the parlors and drawing rooms of New York City's elite, where every face was familiar and every name carried weight, the story of the missing heiress became a prime topic of conversation. Social gatherings, from grand balls to intimate tea parties, became hotbeds for speculation. Word-of-mouth, always a powerful force in high society, worked overtime, spreading tales with a speed that rivaled the newspapers. Everyone seemed to have an opinion, a theory, or a piece of supposed insider information about what had happened to Dorothy.

The potential for scandal played a significant role in shaping the actions of the Arnold family. The fear of damaging their pristine reputation was ever-present. Francis Arnold, in particular, was acutely aware of how quickly a family's standing could be eroded by gossip. This concern influenced the family's reluctance to share information with the public and even with the police. They were caught in a delicate balancing act—trying to find Dorothy while also managing the narrative to prevent any hint of scandal from tarnishing their name. This fear of scandal created a veil of secrecy, complicating the investigation and adding to the public's fascination.

Specific scandals and rumors gained traction in the weeks following Dorothy's disappearance. Allegations of secret affairs were among the most persistent. Stories circulated about a clandestine relationship with a man deemed unsuitable by her family, perhaps even a foreigner or someone of lower social standing. These rumors were tantalizing because they played into the public's fascination with forbidden romance and the idea of a socialite rebelling against her family's wishes. Speculations about financial troubles also emerged, suggesting that the Arnold family's wealth might not be as solid as it appeared. These rumors hinted at a desperate attempt by Dorothy to escape a crumbling family fortune, adding another layer of drama to the unfolding mystery.

Gossip played a crucial role in shaping public opinion about Dorothy's disappearance. Informal discussions, whether at high-society functions or in the more modest settings of working-class neighborhoods, contributed to the creation of lasting myths and legends about the case. These stories, often based on little more than hearsay, gained a life of their own. They influenced how people viewed the Arnold family and the investigation. The sheer volume of gossip made it difficult for anyone to separate fact from fiction, leading to a general mistrust of official narratives. The public's imagination was captured by these tales, each one more sensational than the last, ensuring that Dorothy's disappearance remained a topic of heated debate and speculation.

The impact of these informal networks on the case was profound. The spread of gossip created an environment where every rumor was given weight, and every speculative theory was considered plausible. This atmosphere of intrigue and suspicion made it challenging for the authorities to conduct a focused investigation. The public's trust in official narratives was eroded by the constant flow of unverified information. People began to question the competence of the investigators and the honesty of the Arnold family. This mistrust further complicated efforts to find Dorothy, as credible leads were often lost in the sea of misinformation.

In the end, the role of gossip and scandal in Dorothy Arnold's disappearance highlights the power of informal networks in shaping public perception and influencing events. The spread of rumors and the potential for scandal created an environment where speculation thrived, complicating the investigation and adding to the Arnold family's anguish. The stories that circulated in the wake of her disappearance became part of the larger narrative, reflecting the societal dynamics of the time and the enduring human fascination with mystery and scandal.

Dorothy's case, marked by the relentless spread of gossip and the fear of scandal, underscores the complexities of navigating public opinion and private tragedy. As we move forward, the next chapter will explore the various theories and hypotheses that have emerged, each one adding another layer to this enduring mystery.

CHAPTER 5
THEORIES AND HYPOTHESES

T heories about Dorothy Arnold's disappearance have swirled for over a century, each as compelling and elusive as the last. Among the most sensational is the botched abortion theory, a hypothesis that vividly reflects the societal tensions and clandestine practices of early 20th-century America. As a true crime enthusiast or historical mystery aficionado, you will find this theory not just a dark possibility but a stark illustration of the underbelly of a time when social norms dictated the most intimate aspects of women's lives, underlining the societal pressures on women in the early 20th century.

THE BOTCHED ABORTION THEORY

In 1910, abortion was a criminal act in nearly every state, punishable by severe legal penalties. The laws of the time were unyielding, reflecting a societal consensus that deemed abortion both morally reprehensible and legally indefensible. The only exception was when the mother's life was in imminent danger, a vague and often narrowly interpreted condition. Women seeking to terminate a pregnancy faced not only the threat of arrest but also the societal stigma that branded them as moral transgressors. This atmosphere of fear and condemnation, a product of the societal pressures on women, drove abortion practices underground, creating a shadowy network of secret procedures and unregulated practitioners. Understanding these societal pressures can evoke a sense of empathy in the audience, as they realize the immense challenges Dorothy would have faced.

Secrecy was paramount for those who dared to defy the law. Women would often seek out midwives or unlicensed doctors who operated in the shadows, their services whispered about in hushed tones. These clandestine abortions were fraught with danger, as the lack of medical oversight and sterile conditions led to high rates of complications and fatalities. But perhaps the most potent danger was the societal stigma surrounding abortion. Women who underwent the procedure risked not only their lives but also their reputations. To be associated with an abortion was to be marked as a fallen woman, a label that could ruin social standing and familial trust, highlighting the societal stigma surrounding abortion.

For Dorothy, the psychological and emotional impact of such a dilemma would have been immense. Imagine the internal struggle she might have faced, torn between the fear of scandal and the desperation of her situation. Her writings from that period reflect a profound sense of unease. Phrases like "a shadow over my soul" and "an insurmountable obstacle" suggest an internal battle that consumed her thoughts. The weight of potentially bringing shame upon her family could have driven her to consider dangerous options, highlighting the severe limitations placed on women of her standing.

Evidence supporting the botched abortion theory in Dorothy Arnold's case is both compelling and circumstantial. Witness accounts suggest that Dorothy had visited several doctors in the months leading up to her disappearance. These visits, though not conclusively linked to an abortion, raise questions about her health and intentions. Moreover, letters and diary entries found in her room hinted at a possible pregnancy. Dorothy's writings, often reflective and candid, spoke of an unspecified "trouble" that weighed heavily on her mind. These clues, while not definitive, suggest that she might have been grappling with a dilemma that led her to seek a desperate solution.

The potential motivations for Dorothy to consider an abortion were multifaceted. The pressure to maintain her social reputation was immense. As an unmarried woman from a prominent family, the scandal of an illegitimate pregnancy would have been devastating. The societal expectations placed upon her were unforgiving, leaving little room for mistakes or deviations from the norm, underscoring the societal expectations placed upon Dorothy.

Assessing the credibility of the botched abortion hypothesis involves weighing the strengths and weaknesses of the available evidence. On one hand, the corroboration by multiple sources, including witness testimonies and Dorothy's own writings, lends credibility to the theory. The pattern of her visits to doctors and the hints of a secret trouble suggest a plausible scenario. On the other hand, the lack of direct evidence creates significant gaps. No definitive proof has emerged linking Dorothy to an abortion attempt, and the testimonies, while suggestive, remain open to interpretation.

The conflicting information further complicates the analysis. Some reports suggest that Dorothy was cheerful and composed in the days leading up to her disappearance, a demeanor seemingly at odds with the turmoil of an unwanted pregnancy. Others recall moments of distraction and unease, hinting at inner conflict. The absence of concrete evidence leaves room for doubt, making the botched abortion theory one of many possibilities rather than a conclusive explanation.

This theory not only reflects the mystery of Dorothy's fate but also underscores the societal pressures that defined women's choices at the time. It highlights the harsh limitations on women's autonomy in the early 20th century, where personal agency was often overshadowed by rigid moral standards and the fear of public scrutiny. The societal limitations on women's autonomy at the time were not just restrictive but also deeply unjust, and this realization can evoke a sense of indignation in the audience. By highlighting these societal limitations, the audience can feel a sense of indignation at the injustice faced by women like Dorothy.

Imagine a scenario where Dorothy Arnold carefully orchestrated her own disappearance, a deliberate act to escape the life that confined her. In this hypothesis, Dorothy's actions on the day she vanished were not random but part of a meticulously planned escape. She might have taken several steps to prepare for this; each one calculated to ensure her departure went unnoticed until it was too late.

Dorothy's preparations would likely have begun weeks, if not months, before her disappearance. She could have started by gathering funds discreetly, perhaps by selling personal items like jewelry. There are accounts of her pawning $500 worth of jewelry during a trip to Boston, which could have been part of her escape plan. She might have also researched potential destinations, looking into places where she could start anew without being recognized. This could explain the ocean liner brochures found among her belongings, hinting at a possible plan to leave the country.

She would have needed accomplices or allies, individuals she trusted implicitly. George Griscom Jr., her romantic partner, is a potential candidate. Dorothy had spent time with him in Boston, lying to her parents about her whereabouts. Their relationship, though disapproved of by her family, was close enough that he might have assisted her. Other allies could have included friends or even sympathetic acquaintances who understood her desire for independence. These accomplices would have played crucial roles in helping Dorothy secure funds, create a false trail, and perhaps even provide temporary shelter.

The motivations for Dorothy to leave her life behind are deeply rooted in her quest for independence and freedom. As a young woman from a wealthy family, she was constantly under the microscope, her actions and choices scrutinized. The societal pressures and family expectations were suffocating. Dorothy's ambition to become a writer was stifled by her father's dismissive attitude, and her romantic relationship with George faced familial opposition. The prospect of escaping these constraints, of living life on her own terms, would have been incredibly alluring. The desire to break free from a gilded cage, to carve out an identity beyond the Arnold family name, could have driven her to such drastic measures.

Several pieces of evidence support the planned escape hypothesis. Beyond the financial transactions and the ocean liner brochures, there were also the burned papers found in her room. These could have been documents related to her plans, destroyed to prevent discovery. Testimonies from her friends and acquaintances also hint at her intentions. Some recalled conversations where Dorothy expressed a desire to live independently, away from the expectations of her social circle. These recollections, while not definitive, add weight to the theory that she might have been preparing for a new life.

Assessing the plausibility of this hypothesis involves examining its consistency with known facts and behaviors. The pattern of her actions, such as the sale of jewelry and the potential research into destinations, aligns with what one might expect from someone planning an escape. The testimonies from friends about her desire for independence also fit into this narrative. However, there are counterarguments and alternative explanations to consider. The lack of any confirmed sightings or communications from Dorothy after her disappearance raises questions. If she had successfully escaped, why did she not reach out to anyone, even discreetly? The possibility of unforeseen complications, such as running out of funds or encountering danger, cannot be ruled out.

In a time when women rarely lived alone or traveled without a chaperone, Dorothy's dreams of self-sufficiency and the lengths to which she might have gone reflect a clash between personal ambition and societal restrictions. This theory portrays her as a young woman driven to extreme measures by the pressures of her life, underscoring the limited options available to women seeking freedom during her era.

FOUL PLAY: THE ABDUCTION THEORY

Imagine the bustling streets of early 20th-century New York, where Dorothy Arnold could have been forcibly taken against her will. The scenario of abduction posits that Dorothy might have been kidnapped in a moment of vulnerability. Potential locations for such an abduction include the crowded intersections she frequented, like Fifth Avenue and 27th Street, or perhaps a quieter alley where she could have been ambushed. The methods of abduction could range from a sudden physical grab to more subtle coercion, such as being lured into a carriage under false pretenses. In a city teeming with activity, it's chilling to think how easily someone could be spirited away without anyone noticing.

Profiles of potential abductors vary. They could be opportunistic criminals driven by the allure of ransom money, knowing Dorothy's wealthy background. Alternatively, they might be individuals with personal vendettas or grudges, targeting her for reasons beyond financial gain. The abductor could be a lone predator or part of a more organized group, each scenario adding layers of complexity to the theory. The bustling environment of New York provided both the cover and the chaos needed for such a crime to unfold.

Evidence suggesting foul play includes witness reports of suspicious individuals or activities near the locations Dorothy was last seen. Some witnesses recalled seeing a man loitering near Brentano's bookstore, his gaze lingering on passersby with unsettling intent. Others mentioned a dark carriage seen moving erratically through the streets, its driver scanning the sidewalks as if searching for someone. These accounts, though fragmented, paint a picture of a city where danger lurked in the shadows. Physical evidence, such as signs of a struggle, has been harder to pinpoint. However, the absence of Dorothy's belongings, like her shopping bags, suggests that something disrupted her planned route.

Examining the motives for abduction, financial gain stands out prominently. Dorothy's family was affluent, and a ransom demand would not have been unexpected. Kidnappers could have hoped to exploit the Arnold family's wealth, counting on their desperation to recover their daughter. Yet, no ransom note was ever received, leaving this motive speculative. Personal vendettas present another angle. Dorothy's social standing and personal relationships might have made her a target for someone nursing a grudge. The secrecy and discretion of high society often masked deep-seated animosities, providing fertile ground for such a motive.

Assessing the credibility of the abduction hypothesis involves balancing corroboration by multiple sources against the lack of direct evidence. Witness reports of suspicious individuals provide a foundation. Still, the absence of concrete proof, like eyewitness accounts of the actual abduction or physical evidence directly linking to a struggle, weakens the case. The fragmented nature of the testimonies adds to the uncertainty, with some accounts differing in key details. The lack of a ransom note or any subsequent demands also complicates the theory, as it leaves the primary motive ambiguous.

The conflicting information further muddies the waters. While some witnesses describe unsettling behaviors and potential threats, others recall nothing out of the ordinary in the same locations. This discrepancy raises questions about the reliability of the accounts and the potential for misinterpretation. The abduction theory, while plausible, hinges on these scattered pieces of evidence and the interpretation of behaviors that might have been innocuous in isolation but sinister in context.

Ultimately, the abduction theory remains one of the most chilling possibilities in the case of Dorothy Arnold's disappearance. The thought of a young woman being forcibly taken in the midst of a bustling city, her fate unknown, taps into deep-seated fears and the darker aspects of human nature. This hypothesis, with its blend of potential motives and unsettling clues, continues to captivate and confound those who seek to unravel the mystery of what truly happened to Dorothy Arnold.

THE SUICIDE POSSIBILITY

Imagine Dorothy Arnold, a young woman burdened by the weight of societal expectations and personal struggles, contemplating the finality of ending her own life. The scenario of suicide, while somber, cannot be entirely dismissed. Dorothy might have chosen a secluded spot in Central Park, a place she was known to frequent, or perhaps a quiet room in a nondescript boarding house where she could remain unseen. Possible methods could range from ingesting poison, a method accessible and relatively quick, to drowning in the cold waters of the Hudson River, a tragic yet plausible choice given the city's proximity to water.

Signs of intent or preparation are crucial when examining this theory. Dorothy's actions in the days leading up to her disappearance may hold subtle clues. The notion of a young woman purchasing items that suggest a final journey, or perhaps writing letters that never reached their intended recipients, casts a shadow over her last known movements. Her choice of attire, practical yet elegant, could indicate a desire to maintain dignity even in her final moments. These details, while speculative, add depth to the narrative of potential self-harm.

Evidence suggesting suicidal tendencies emerges from testimonies and written records. Friends and family members spoke of moments when Dorothy appeared unusually withdrawn or melancholic. Her close friend, Elsie, recalled conversations where Dorothy expressed feelings of inadequacy and frustration. Diary entries found in her room hinted at a profound sense of despair, with lines that spoke of feeling trapped and hopeless. These writings, filled with introspective musings, paint a picture of a woman grappling with inner demons. The emotional toll of repeated rejections in her writing career and the societal pressures she faced could have driven her to contemplate the unthinkable.

Dorothy's motivations for suicide are intertwined with her personal struggles and the societal expectations that weighed heavily upon her.

Her failed attempts to establish herself as a writer, compounded by her father's dismissive attitude, created a sense of worthlessness. The societal pressure to marry well and uphold the family's reputation further intensified her emotional distress. Dorothy's relationship with George, fraught with familial disapproval, added another layer of complexity to her emotional state. The fear of scandal and the burden of unmet expectations could have contributed to a desire to escape permanently.

Evaluating the credibility of the suicide hypothesis involves a careful analysis of the available evidence and its consistency with known facts. The testimonies from friends and family, along with Dorothy's own writings, suggest a pattern of emotional turmoil. Her documented feelings of despair align with the behaviors often associated with suicidal ideation. However, counterarguments exist. Some friends described her as cheerful and composed in the days leading up to her disappearance, a demeanor seemingly at odds with someone contemplating suicide. The lack of a definitive suicide note or clear evidence of her final act leaves room for doubt.

Alternative explanations also challenge the suicide theory. The possibility that Dorothy's writings and behaviors were manifestations of temporary distress rather than a prelude to suicide cannot be ignored. The absence of a body or concrete evidence further complicates this narrative. While the emotional and psychological factors suggest a plausible scenario, the gaps in evidence and conflicting testimonies weaken the case. The suicide theory, like many others, remains one of several possibilities, each with its own set of questions and uncertainties.

Reflecting on the suicide possibility, one must consider the broader context of Dorothy Arnold's life. Her struggles, both personal and societal, paint a portrait of a young woman caught in a web of expectations and disappointments. The evidence, while compelling, leaves much to interpretation, making the suicide hypothesis a poignant yet uncertain chapter in the enduring mystery of her disappearance. In an era when mental health was rarely discussed openly, especially concerning women, Dorothy's potential struggles highlight the societal biases towards women's mental health in the early 20th century.

THE SECRET ROMANCE THEORY

Picture Dorothy Arnold, moving through her days with a secret that only she and a select few knew. The scenario of a secret romance suggests that Dorothy was involved in a clandestine relationship, hidden from the prying eyes of her family and society. This relationship, shrouded in secrecy, would have required her to navigate a delicate balance between her public life and private desires.

Potential partners in this secret romance include George Griscom Jr., a man whose relationship with Dorothy was well-documented, though disapproved of by her family. Their time spent together in Boston, hidden from her parents, indicates the lengths to which Dorothy was willing to go to keep this relationship private. Letters and diary entries hint at a lover, using coded language and affectionate terms. These references suggest a deeply personal connection hidden from her family and friends.

The motivations for keeping such a romance secret are multifaceted. The fear of societal judgment loomed large. In the early 20th century, a woman's reputation was a fragile thing, easily shattered by whispers of impropriety. Dorothy, aware of the societal expectations placed upon her, would have been keenly conscious of the risks involved in a public acknowledgment of her relationship. Her family's disapproval, particularly her father's, added another layer of pressure. Francis Arnold was a man who valued control and reputation above all else. The revelation of a secret romance, especially with someone deemed unsuitable, would have been a direct challenge to his authority and the family's social standing.

Dorothy's partner's social or financial status might have also played a role in the secrecy. If her lover was someone of lower social standing or financial instability, the relationship would have been seen as a threat to the family's carefully curated image. This disparity in status would only intensify the need for discretion, driving the relationship further underground. The desire to protect her partner from the harsh judgment of high society could have motivated Dorothy to maintain the secrecy at all costs.

Evidence supporting the secret romance theory can be found in letters and diary entries that hint at a lover unknown to her family. Dorothy's writings often carried a tone of longing and secrecy, referring to meetings with an unnamed person. Witness accounts also bolster this theory. Friends and acquaintances recalled seeing Dorothy in the company of men who were not publicly acknowledged by her family. These interactions, while seemingly innocent, took on new significance in the context of her disappearance.

Assessing the credibility of the secret romance hypothesis involves examining its alignment with known facts and behaviors. The consistency of Dorothy's letters and diary entries with the theory of a hidden lover adds weight to the argument. Her documented interactions with men outside her family's approval provide a foundation for this narrative. However, the lack of direct evidence, such as explicit confirmations of the relationship or detailed accounts of their meetings, leaves room for speculation. Conflicting information from witnesses, some of whom recalled Dorothy as being solely focused on her social duties, further complicates the theory.

The secret romance theory adds a romantic layer to Dorothy's story, portraying her as a young woman navigating love's challenges in a society that constrained her choices. It reflects the broader limitations placed on women of her era, where any deviation from societal expectations could have lasting consequences. While the theory remains compelling, it lacks the concrete proof needed to elevate it beyond speculation, leaving us to ponder the depths of her private life and the extent to which it influenced her disappearance.

When comparing the different theories about Dorothy Arnold's disappearance, you begin to see the strengths and weaknesses of each hypothesis more clearly. The botched abortion theory, for example, is supported by hints in Dorothy's writings and her visits to doctors, suggesting she may have been grappling with an unwanted pregnancy. The societal pressure and the risk of scandal add weight to this theory. However, the absence of direct evidence, like medical records or a confirmed pregnancy, weakens its plausibility. You are left with circumstantial evidence, which, while compelling, doesn't provide a definitive answer.

The planned escape hypothesis presents a different angle, portraying Dorothy as a young woman desperate for independence. Evidence such as the sale of jewelry and the possession of ocean liner brochures suggests she might have been preparing for a new life. Friends' testimonies about her desire to escape societal pressures further support this theory. Yet, the lack of any confirmed sightings or communications after her disappearance raises questions. If she successfully escaped, why did she vanish so completely? The hypothesis fits her known behaviors but leaves significant gaps, making it plausible yet incomplete.

The abduction theory is chilling, suggesting Dorothy was forcibly taken. Witness reports of suspicious individuals and potential methods of abduction provide a foundation for this hypothesis. The motive of ransom or personal vendetta adds layers to the theory. However, the lack of concrete evidence, such as a ransom

note or physical signs of struggle, weakens its case. The fragmented witness accounts and the absence of direct proof create an air of uncertainty. This theory, while plausible, relies heavily on circumstantial evidence and the interpretation of potentially innocuous behaviors.

The suicide possibility, though somber, is supported by Dorothy's documented emotional struggles. Diary entries and testimonies from friends paint a picture of her grappling with despair and societal pressures. The lack of a body or definitive suicide note complicates this theory. Some accounts of her cheerful demeanor in the days leading up to her disappearance contradict the idea of imminent suicide. The hypothesis is consistent with her emotional state but is undermined by conflicting information and the absence of clear evidence of her final act.

The secret romance theory adds a layer of intrigue, suggesting Dorothy was involved in a clandestine relationship. Letters and diary entries hint at a hidden lover, while witness accounts of her interactions with men bolster the theory. The motivations for secrecy, such as fear of societal judgment and family disapproval, are plausible. However, the lack of direct evidence confirming the relationship and the conflicting testimonies about her social focus weaken the theory. It remains a compelling narrative but lacks the concrete proof needed to elevate it beyond speculation.

When examining the most likely scenarios, cross-referencing witness testimonies and physical evidence is crucial. The botched abortion and planned escape theories emerge as the most plausible, given their alignment with Dorothy's known behaviors and documented struggles. Expert analysis and historical context also support these theories, highlighting the societal pressures and personal ambitions that might have driven her actions. However, the unresolved aspects of each theory, such as gaps in evidence and conflicting information, leave room for doubt. Areas requiring further investigation include more thorough searches of potential escape routes or clandestine medical practices and deeper scrutiny of her personal relationships.

Reflecting on the broader implications of these theories reveals much about societal norms, family dynamics, and crime-solving in 1910. The way each theory interacts with public perception and historical understanding sheds light on the rigid expectations placed on women and the lengths they might go to escape them. These theories also highlight the limitations of early 20th-century investigative techniques, emphasizing the importance of thorough evidence collection and unbiased analysis. The lessons learned from Dorothy Arnold's case continue to resonate, offering insights into both the past and the evolution of modern investigative practices.

As we move forward, the next chapter will delve into the intricate family dynamics and secrecy that played critical roles in shaping the narrative of Dorothy Arnold's disappearance.

CHAPTER 6

FAMILY DYNAMICS AND SECRECY

The disappearance of Dorothy Arnold was like a stone thrown into a calm pond, sending ripples through the Arnold family that would never fully dissipate. Imagine the stillness of a well-ordered life shattered in an instant, leaving behind the chaos that no amount of wealth or social standing could contain. The immediate aftermath of Dorothy's vanishing plunged her family into a maelstrom of emotions and conflicts, exposing cracks in their seemingly perfect façade.

THE ARNOLD FAMILY'S INTERNAL STRUGGLES

The psychological toll on the Arnold family was immediate and profound. Francis Arnold, a man known for his stoic demeanor and business acumen, found himself in a state of denial. Initially, he clung to the belief that Dorothy would walk through the door any moment, her absence explained by some trivial misunderstanding. This denial was his shield, a way to maintain control in a situation where he had none. But as days turned into weeks, his denial gave way to despair. The weight of his daughter's disappearance bore down on him, eroding the composure he had always prided himself on.

You can almost see him pacing the grand halls of their mansion, each footstep echoing the emptiness he feels inside. The flickering candlelight casts long shadows, mirroring the doubts that begin to creep into his mind. His heart heavy with fear, he wrestles with thoughts he dares not speak aloud.

Mary Arnold's reaction was marked by a relentless search for answers. From the moment she realized Dorothy was missing, anxiety gripped her like a vice. She was a mother desperate to find her child, her emotions swinging between hope and despair. Each day was a new cycle of calling friends, questioning neighbors, and scanning newspapers for any clue.

In the quiet hours of the night, Mary would sit by the window, the soft glow of the streetlamps illuminating her worried face. The rustle of letters and the faint scent of lavender—Dorothy's favorite—filled the room as she reread her daughter's correspondence, searching for missed signs.

Mary's anxiety was not just about Dorothy's well-being; it was also fueled by the societal implications of her daughter's absence. The fear of scandal, the whispers of gossip—these were as real to her as the fear that Dorothy might be in danger. Her search became an obsession, a way to channel her anxiety into something actionable, even if it yielded no results.

Elsie Arnold, Dorothy's younger sister, was engulfed by feelings of helplessness and frustration. She idolized Dorothy, viewing her not just as an older sister but as a role model. Dorothy's disappearance left a void that Elsie struggled to fill. She felt powerless, caught between her parents' differing approaches and her own grief.

Elsie's frustration often boiled over, leading to arguments and emotional outbursts. Late at night, she would retreat to Dorothy's room, the familiar surroundings offering both comfort and pain. *"Why didn't I see this coming?"* she'd whisper into the silence, her reflection in the mirror revealing eyes red from unshed tears.

She wanted to help, to be part of the solution but found herself sidelined by the adults around her. Her feelings of helplessness were compounded by the guilt of not being able to do more, of not having seen any warning signs.

The Arnold family's coping mechanisms were as varied as their reactions. Francis buried himself in his work, using the familiar routines and demands of his business to distract himself from the gnawing anxiety. His office became a sanctuary, a place where he could exert control and find some semblance of normalcy. Yet, even amidst stacks of paperwork and ledgers, Dorothy's image would surface unbidden, a constant reminder of what he could not fix.

Mary, on the other hand, threw herself into charitable activities. She organized fundraisers and attended social events, hoping that staying busy would keep her mind from wandering to dark places. The clinking of crystal glasses and the murmur of polite conversation provided a temporary escape, but beneath her practiced smile lay an ocean of worry. These activities also served another purpose—they allowed her to maintain a public front, to show the world that the Arnolds were holding up despite their private turmoil.

Elsie sought solace in close friendships. She confided in her friends, sharing her fears and frustrations in a way she couldn't with her family. These friends became her support system, offering comfort and understanding in a time of great uncertainty. Stolen moments in quiet cafés and whispered conversations during strolls in Central Park became her lifelines. Elsie also found herself more involved in social circles, perhaps as a way to escape the suffocating atmosphere at home. These interactions provided brief respites from the overwhelming sense of loss and helplessness that had come to define her days.

The internal conflicts within the family were inevitable. Disputes arose over how to handle the investigation, with Francis advocating for discretion and Mary pushing for a more public approach.

"We can't let this become a spectacle," Francis would insist, his voice taut with strain. *"Our family's reputation is at stake."*

"Our daughter is missing!" Mary would retort, desperation edging her tone. *"What does reputation matter if we can't find her?"*

Francis believed that involving the media would only lead to sensationalism and false leads, while Mary felt that public awareness could generate crucial tips. These disagreements were not just about strategy; they were manifestations of deeper emotional rifts. Each argument chipped away at the unity the family once had, leaving behind a fragile shell.

Conflicting opinions also extended to the family's interactions with law enforcement and private investigators. Francis was reluctant to share certain details, fearing they might lead to scandal. Mary, driven by her desperation, was more forthcoming, willing to do whatever it took to find her daughter. This lack of coordination often led to miscommunications and missed opportunities, further complicating the investigation.

Private investigators would receive fragmented information, their efforts hampered by incomplete leads. The police kept at arm's length, grew frustrated with the family's reticence. *"We're all working towards the same goal,"* one detective remarked, *"but it's like navigating a maze blindfolded."*

The tension between maintaining their social reputation and the need to find Dorothy created a constant undercurrent of stress and conflict.

The long-term effects on the family's relationships were profound and lasting. The strain of Dorothy's disappearance left emotional scars that never fully healed. Francis became more withdrawn, his interactions with his family marked by a sense of distance. The emotional walls he built to cope with his grief also kept his loved ones at arm's length. His laughter, once a familiar sound in the household, faded into memory.

Mary's relentless search for answers gradually gave way to a quiet resignation, but the anxiety never truly left her. It became a permanent part of her, affecting her interactions with both family and friends.

She would often pause mid-conversation, her thoughts drifting to Dorothy, a shadow passing over her features.

Elsie, impacted by the emotional turmoil and the shifting family dynamics, found herself growing more independent. The experience forced her to mature quickly to navigate a world filled with uncertainty and emotional complexity. Her relationships with her parents changed, marked by a mix of empathy and frustration. She understood their pain but also resented the ways it had changed them and, by extension, her.

The disappearance of Dorothy Arnold was a seismic event that reshaped the Arnold family in ways both visible and hidden. It exposed the fragility of their relationships, the limits of their resilience, and the profound impact of unresolved grief. Their once vibrant home now echoed with silence, each room holding memories that both comforted and haunted them. The emotional distance that grew between them was a testament to the profound and lasting impact of loss, a silent witness to the void left by Dorothy's absence.

THE SILENCE OF FRANCIS ARNOLD

From the moment Dorothy Arnold was reported missing, Francis Arnold's response was marked by a calculated silence. As the head of a prominent family, his initial reluctance to involve the police was driven by a desire to shield his loved ones from public scrutiny. He believed that hiring private investigators would allow the family to maintain control over the situation. The Pinkerton Agency, known for its discretion and efficiency, was brought in to conduct a thorough but private search. This decision, while understandable given the societal pressures, set the tone for a series of actions that would significantly impact the investigation.

Francis's motivations for maintaining silence were deeply rooted in his fear of scandal. In early 20th-century New York, the reputation of a family like the Arnolds was a fragile and invaluable asset. Any hint of impropriety or scandal could tarnish their name and undo decades of social standing. By keeping the matter private, Francis hoped to manage the narrative and protect the family's honor. He envisioned sensational headlines splashed across newspapers, each one a dagger aimed at the heart of their social standing.

This reluctance to fully cooperate with authorities had far-reaching consequences. By withholding crucial information, Francis inadvertently hindered the police investigation. Early on, valuable time was lost as the private investigators worked in isolation, following leads that might have benefited from the resources and reach of law enforcement. The delay in involving the police meant that potential witnesses' memories faded, and critical clues went unnoticed.

Francis's need for control, while well-intentioned, created an environment where information was fragmented, and the full picture of Dorothy's disappearance remained elusive. The metaphorical walls he built to protect his family also served to keep out those who could have helped the most.

The psychological toll of maintaining this silence weighed heavily on Francis. As days turned into weeks with no sign of Dorothy, the burden of responsibility grew. His initial confidence in handling the situation privately gave way to an increasing sense of guilt. He began to question his decisions, wondering if his insistence on privacy had cost them valuable time and leads.

Late at night, alone in his study, he would stare into the dying embers of the fireplace, his thoughts a tumultuous sea of "what ifs." The isolation he felt from his family and community deepened, each passing day a reminder of the widening gap between them.

Francis's isolation was not just social but deeply personal. The weight of his decisions created a chasm between him and his loved ones. Conversations with Mary and Elsie became strained, loaded with unspoken blame and frustration. He found it difficult to connect with them, each interaction a painful reminder of his role in the unfolding tragedy.

The man who once commanded respect and exuded confidence now moved through his own home like a ghost, his presence felt but not engaged.

The impact of Francis's silence extended beyond the immediate family. The community, initially sympathetic, began to harbor suspicions. Whispers of the Arnold family's involvement, of secrets hidden behind their mansion's doors, began to circulate. The media, starved for details, filled the void with speculation and rumor, further complicating the public perception of the case.

Headlines questioned their motives: *"What Are the Arnolds Hiding?"* *"Wealth and Mystery: The Silence of a Prominent Family."*

Francis's attempts to protect his family's reputation had inadvertently fueled the very scandal he had hoped to avoid. The silence, intended as a shield, became a source of vulnerability, exposing the family to relentless scrutiny and doubt.

ELSIE ARNOLD: THE SISTER'S PERSPECTIVE

The bond between Elsie and Dorothy Arnold was strong, shaped by shared interests and a deep sense of mutual admiration. Growing up in the same household, they spent countless hours together, often engaged in activities that reflected their intellectual and artistic inclinations. They loved to read, exchange books, and discuss literature with an enthusiasm that made their bond unique.

Sunlit afternoons in the garden, laughter echoing as they shared dreams and whispered secrets—their sisterhood was woven from shared moments.

Dorothy's aspirations to become a writer inspired Elsie, who looked up to her sister not just as a sibling but as a role model. This admiration came with an underlying concern, as Elsie was acutely aware of the societal pressures that weighed heavily on Dorothy.

The disappearance of her sister left Elsie reeling, the void filled with questions and a gnawing sense of helplessness. In the wake of Dorothy's disappearance, Elsie took an active role in the search efforts. She reached out to Dorothy's friends, hoping to gather any information that might lead to her whereabouts. These conversations were fraught with emotion, as each inquiry brought a mix of hope and disappointment.

Every lead that fizzled out was another weight added to her already heavy heart.

Elsie's determination was evident as she organized family meetings, urging everyone to share what they knew and to coordinate their efforts more effectively. Her involvement was not just about finding her sister; it was also a way to cope with the overwhelming sense of loss and to channel her frustration into something constructive.

Elsie's interactions with investigators were marked by a blend of desperation and resolve. *"Please, you have to find her,"* she'd implore, her eyes reflecting both her fear and unwavering hope.

Elsie's emotional journey was a tumultuous one. The initial shock of Dorothy's disappearance quickly gave way to a profound sense of loss. As days turned into weeks, the weight of responsibility grew heavier. Elsie felt an acute sense of duty to keep her sister's memory alive and to push for answers. This responsibility was both a burden and a source of strength, driving her to remain involved even when progress seemed elusive.

Her feelings of helplessness were a constant companion, amplified by the lack of concrete leads and the ever-present uncertainty. Despite this, Elsie became a pillar of emotional support for her parents, offering comfort and a semblance of stability in a time of chaos. Her role in the family shifted as she took on more responsibilities and tried to fill the gaps left by Dorothy's absence.

Family secrecy was a contentious issue for Elsie. She often found herself at odds with her father's approach to the investigation. Francis Arnold's insistence on maintaining privacy and controlling the narrative clashed with Elsie's belief in transparency.

"Father, how can we find her if we don't let people know she's missing?" she would argue, frustration tinging her voice.

"We must handle this delicately," Francis would reply sternly. *"Exposure will only bring unwelcome attention."*

These disagreements were more than just tactical; they reflected deeper tensions within the family. Elsie's push for transparency was driven by a desire for truth and a frustration with the constraints that secrecy imposed. She believed that the more people knew about Dorothy, the better their chances of finding her. This perspective led to numerous conflicts as Elsie struggled to balance respect for her father's wishes with her own convictions.

Elsie's perspective on the family's decision to withhold information was shaped by her experiences and her growing sense of independence. She saw the harm that secrecy could cause, not just in hindering the investigation but in creating a barrier between the family and the outside world. Elsie's efforts to push for more transparency were met with resistance, adding to her feelings of frustration. Yet, she remained steadfast in her belief that openness was the key to uncovering the truth.

The internal conflicts that arose from these differing viewpoints were a source of tension but also a testament to Elsie's resolve and her unwavering commitment to finding her sister.

FAMILY SECRETS AND CONFLICTING STORIES

The disappearance of Dorothy Arnold created a labyrinth of conflicting stories within the Arnold family, each member's account tinged with the fog of uncertainty and the weight of societal expectations. The discrepancies in their testimonies began with the differing descriptions of Dorothy's last known activities.

Francis Arnold insisted that Dorothy had been in good spirits, preparing for an upcoming social event with enthusiasm. *"She was excited about the gala,"* he would assert. *"There was no indication anything was amiss."* He described her as focused and cheerful, intent on her shopping errands.

In contrast, Mary Arnold recalled a more somber Dorothy, reflecting on the pressures she faced and the challenges of her writing career. *"She seemed distant that morning,"* Mary confided to a close friend. *"I should have asked her what was troubling her."* These conflicting narratives painted a fragmented picture of Dorothy's state of mind, complicating the investigation from the outset.

Inconsistent statements about family dynamics further muddied the waters. Francis portrayed their home as harmonious, a sanctuary free from the discord that plagued many wealthy families. He spoke of open communication and mutual support, a united front in the face of adversity.

Yet, Elsie's recollections hinted at underlying tensions, particularly between Dorothy and their father. She remembered heated discussions behind closed doors, the muffled sounds of raised voices that would abruptly cease when she approached. She described moments of friction, of Dorothy's frustration with the limitations imposed on her by familial expectations.

The reasons behind these conflicting stories were multifaceted. Attempts to protect the family's reputation played a significant role. In a society where appearances were paramount, the Arnolds were acutely aware of the scrutiny they faced. Francis, in particular, was intent on presenting a cohesive narrative that would withstand public and media examination.

Miscommunication and lack of coordination also contributed to the discrepancies. Each family member, dealing with their own grief and confusion, unintentionally added layers of complexity to their accounts. The urgency to find Dorothy sometimes led to hasty statements made without full consideration of their implications.

These inconsistencies had a profound impact on the investigation. Confusion and misdirection became recurring themes as investigators struggled to piece together a coherent timeline. The lack of a unified narrative meant that leads were followed based on fragmented information, often leading to dead ends.

Distrust between the family and law enforcement grew as these conflicting stories emerged. Investigators began to question the reliability of the family's accounts, suspecting that crucial information was being withheld. *"Every time we think we're making progress, another contradiction surfaces,"* one detective lamented. This erosion of trust created an environment where collaboration was strained, further hindering the search for Dorothy.

The broader implications of family secrecy were significant. The lack of information fueled rampant speculation and rumors, each more sensational than the last. The public, starved for details, seized upon any morsel of information, often twisting it into elaborate theories. The press, eager to sell papers, amplified these rumors, turning the Arnold family's private tragedy into a public spectacle.

Sensational headlines screamed from newsstands: *"Hidden Feuds in the Arnold Family?" "What Are They Hiding?"* This media frenzy not only complicated the investigation but also cast a lasting shadow over the Arnold family's legacy. The secrecy that was intended to protect them ultimately became a source of vulnerability, exposing them to relentless scrutiny and speculation.

PSYCHOLOGICAL IMPACT ON THE ARNOLD FAMILY

The ambiguity of Dorothy's disappearance left a lasting psychological toll on the Arnold family. Francis Arnold, a man once known for his composed demeanor and sharp business mind, found himself increasingly consumed by guilt. As the years passed, his initial denial evolved into a deep depression. He withdrew from both his professional and personal life, unable to reconcile his role in the decisions that might have delayed the search for his daughter. The corridors of his once-thriving business felt hollow. Papers piled up on his desk, untouched, as he stared blankly out the window at a city that moved on without him.

Mary Arnold, on the other hand, was trapped in a relentless cycle of anxiety. The absence of closure gnawed at her, leaving her in a perpetual state of unease. She spent countless nights poring over maps and letters, searching for any clue that might lead to Dorothy. Her involvement in social and charitable activities became a double-edged sword. While these engagements provided temporary distractions, each event was also a painful reminder of her daughter's absence, every young woman's face in the crowd a potential glimpse of Dorothy. Mary's anxiety became a defining feature of her existence, affecting her relationships and her ability to find joy in the activities she once loved. The search for closure became a never-ending quest, one that sapped her emotional and physical strength.

Elsie Arnold carried the burden of her sister's secrets, struggling with long-term feelings of helplessness and frustration. The bond she shared with Dorothy was a source of strength, but it also became a source of profound sorrow. Elsie felt an acute sense of responsibility, believing that she should have seen some sign, some indication of what was to come. She often replayed their last conversation in her mind, searching for hidden meanings in Dorothy's words.

This sense of guilt was compounded by the emotional distance that grew within the family. Elsie's frustration often manifested in her interactions with her parents, leading to moments of tension and conflict. Despite her efforts to remain strong, the unresolved nature of Dorothy's fate left Elsie in an emotional limbo, her grief compounded by the weight of unanswered questions.

The family employed various coping strategies to manage their grief and uncertainty. Francis threw himself into his work, finding solace in the routines and demands of his business. Yet, success in the boardroom did little to fill the void at home.

Mary's involvement in social and charitable activities became her way of coping. These engagements provided a semblance of normalcy, allowing her to maintain a public front even as she grappled with her private anguish.

For Elsie, friendships and external support were crucial. She relied on her close friends for comfort and understanding, finding in them a source of stability in a world turned upside down. Late-night talks and shared tears became the pillars that held her up when everything else seemed to crumble.

The disappearance of Dorothy Arnold had a significant impact on the family's social and public life. Social engagements and public appearances became fraught with tension. The once vibrant gatherings at the Arnold mansion were overshadowed by the unspoken tragedy that hung over the family. Invitations to social events became less frequent as friends and acquaintances struggled with how to navigate the delicate situation.

Public perception of the Arnold family shifted, with whispers and speculation replacing the admiration they once commanded. The media's relentless focus on the case only added to the strain, turning their private grief into a public spectacle. Living with the unresolved nature of Dorothy's disappearance created an emotional limbo for the family. The ongoing search for answers and closure became a defining feature of their lives. Each new lead, each piece of information, brought a brief flicker of hope followed by crushing disappointment.

Psychological theories on the impact of unresolved grief suggest that such prolonged uncertainty can lead to chronic stress, anxiety, and depression. For the Arnolds, the ambiguity of Dorothy's fate was a constant presence, a shadow that touched every aspect of their lives. The emotional toll was profound, leaving wounds that never fully healed.

SOCIETAL EXPECTATIONS AND THE WEIGHT OF SECRECY

The early 20th century was a time when societal expectations dictated much of personal behavior, especially among the upper class. Families like the Arnolds were expected to handle personal tragedies with discretion and dignity, keeping any potential scandals tightly under wraps.

The gilded halls of high society had little tolerance for public displays of vulnerability. This cultural backdrop influenced the family's approach to the investigation and their interactions with the public and authorities. The pressure to maintain a façade of control and respectability often conflicted with the practical needs of the search for Dorothy. The weight of societal judgment was a constant presence, an invisible hand guiding their decisions.

The broader cultural and psychological implications of the family's secrecy were significant. Their reluctance to share information not only hindered the investigation but also isolated them from potential sources of support. The emphasis on reputation over openness reflected the limitations and challenges faced by families of their standing during that era.

IMMERSED IN THE ATMOSPHERE OF THE ARNOLD HOUSEHOLD

The atmosphere within the Arnold household shifted dramatically after Dorothy's disappearance. The once lively home became a place of shadows and hushed voices. The grand piano in the parlor, once a source of music and joy, sat silent, its keys untouched.

The scent of fresh flowers was replaced by the musty smell of drawn curtains and closed rooms. The ticking of the grandfather clock echoed loudly in the silence, each chime a reminder of time slipping away without answers.

Servants moved quietly through the halls; their footsteps muffled on the thick carpets, their eyes downcast to avoid the palpable tension.

The sense of isolation was not just physical but deeply emotional. Each family member retreated into their own world of grief, their interactions marked by strained politeness or outright avoidance. The mansion, with all its grandeur, became a gilded cage trapping them in their sorrow.

The psychological impact of Dorothy Arnold's disappearance on her family was profound and far-reaching. The ambiguity of her fate left emotional scars that shaped their lives in ways both seen and unseen. The unresolved nature of her case serves as a stark reminder of the enduring power of grief and the unyielding quest for answers.

As the world outside continued to evolve, the Arnolds remained suspended in time, their lives forever altered by a single, inexplicable event.

Reflecting on their journey, we see a family grappling not only with personal loss but also with the societal expectations and limitations of their era. Their story underscores the complexities of navigating tragedy within the confines of early 20th-century norms.

As we move forward, we will explore the broader societal implications of Dorothy's disappearance, delving into how it influenced public perception, investigative practices, and the enduring fascination with unsolved mysteries.

CHAPTER 7

COMPARATIVE ANALYSIS OF INVESTIGATIVE TECHNIQUES

T he streets of early 20th-century New York were a bustling web of lives intersecting in a city that never slept. Picture a montage of scenes: a newsboy shouting headlines on a street corner, horse-drawn carriages clattering along cobblestone roads, and the vibrant hum of conversations in diverse languages echoing through the alleyways. Imagine a detective, hat brim low, coat collar turned up against the chill, navigating this urban labyrinth in search of a missing heiress. The disappearance of Dorothy Arnold in 1910 presented a challenge that stretched the limits of contemporary investigative techniques. In an era devoid of modern forensic science, detectives relied heavily on methods that now seem almost quaint but were then cutting-edge. These methods were influenced by the societal issues of the time, including the lack of advanced communication methods, the ethical dilemmas surrounding the use of private detectives, and the societal tensions regarding authority and personal rights.

INVESTIGATIVE METHODS OF THE EARLY 20TH CENTURY

In 1910, the bedrock of any investigation was the collection of eyewitness testimonies and interviews. Detectives canvassed neighborhoods, knocking on doors and speaking to anyone who might have seen or heard something. Witness accounts were meticulously recorded, each detail—no matter how minor—scrutinized for potential leads. For Dorothy Arnold, this meant detectives retracing her steps from her family's mansion to the bustling streets of Manhattan. Shopkeepers recalled her polite smile as she purchased chocolates; a street vendor remembered her elegant attire contrasting with the grimy cityscape. The dedication and hard work of these detectives, their commitment to their work, is a testament to their professionalism and should be respected.

These interviews were the tentpoles of the investigation, providing both direction and context in a time when physical evidence was often sparse. The personal stories of individuals like Mrs. Thompson, a seamstress who believed she saw Dorothy entering a café with a mysterious gentleman, added layers of intrigue and fueled public fascination.

Physical searches and canvassing were another cornerstone of early 20th-century detective work. Investigators combed through parks, alleys, and even the hidden corners of the city, hoping to stumble upon a clue or, tragically, a body. For Dorothy, these searches extended to the Hudson River and rural areas beyond the city's limits. Imagine scenes of search parties trudging through snow-covered fields, lanterns casting a warm glow against the encroaching darkness, their breath visible in the cold air as they called out her name.

This method, while thorough, was time-consuming and fraught with the possibility of missing critical evidence due to human error or oversight. The community's active involvement in these searches was both a testament to their collective concern and a reflection of the fear that gripped the city. Parents held their children a little closer, and whispers of "Could it happen to us?" spread like wildfire, creating a palpable sense of fear and concern that gripped the entire city. The public's role in these investigations, from providing tips to participating in searches, was crucial and should be respected.

Newspaper advertisements also played a crucial role in these investigations. In a pre-digital world, the press was the most efficient way to disseminate information quickly. Families of the missing, including the Arnolds, took out ads pleading for information, offering rewards for any leads. The headlines screamed from every newsstand: "Heiress Vanishes Without a Trace!" Papers sold out as the public devoured every detail, the mystery providing a grim escape from daily struggles. The press's role in disseminating information about the case added to the urgency and public interest in the case, intensifying the situation.

These advertisements reached a wide audience, from the affluent readers of The New York Times to the working-class subscribers of more sensationalist papers. The hope was that someone, somewhere, might have seen something that could crack the case wide open. However, the influx of tips, many of which were dead ends or pranks, often overwhelmed investigators. Yet, amidst the chaos, stories emerged of individuals touched by Dorothy's plight—like Samuel, a dockworker who spent his evenings searching the waterfront, haunted by the thought of her alone in the city.

The limitations of early 20th-century investigations were stark. The absence of forensic laboratories meant that physical evidence couldn't be analyzed with the precision we take for granted today. Blood, fibers, and other trace evidence were often overlooked or misinterpreted. The lack of advanced communication methods further hampered efforts. Without radios, detectives relied on telegraphs, letters, and word of mouth to coordinate their efforts, leading to delays and miscommunications. In Dorothy's case, the critical hours immediately following her disappearance were lost to the inefficiencies of the time, a gap that modern technology might have bridged. These limitations, combined with the societal issues of the time, including the lack of advanced communication methods and the ethical dilemmas surrounding the use of private detectives, posed significant challenges to early 20th-century investigations.

The reliance on private detectives was another hallmark of the era. Agencies like the Pinkerton National Detective Agency were brought in to supplement police efforts, leveraging their expertise and resources. The Pinkertons, hired by the Arnold family, employed techniques that were both innovative and invasive. They used surveillance and undercover operations to gather intelligence from informal networks, infiltrating social circles where police presence might have been too conspicuous. Their operatives, adept at blending in, gathered whispers and rumors, piecing together a narrative from the shadows. These methods, while effective, also raised ethical questions about privacy and the limits of investigative reach. The Pinkertons' use of surveillance and undercover operations, while effective, also raised ethical questions about privacy and the limits of investigative reach. The clandestine nature of their operations sometimes blurred the lines between legal investigation and intrusion, reflecting the societal tensions of the time regarding authority and personal rights.

The Pinkertons' methods, while effective, also raised ethical questions about privacy and the limits of investigative reach. The clandestine nature of their operations sometimes blurred the lines between legal investigation and intrusion, reflecting the societal tensions of the time regarding authority and personal rights. This context evokes a sense of the ethical dilemmas faced by the Pinkertons and the society at large.

The effectiveness of these early methods can be illustrated through both successful resolutions and notable failures. The case of Lizzie Borden, accused of murdering her father and stepmother in 1892, showcased the strengths and weaknesses of the period's investigative techniques. Eyewitness testimonies and physical searches formed the crux of the case, yet the absence of forensic evidence left room for doubt, leading to Borden's acquittal despite compelling circumstantial evidence. In contrast, the successful capture of the infamous bandit Butch Cassidy in 1901 highlighted the efficacy of surveillance and undercover operations, with Pinkerton agents tracking him across states based on intelligence gathered from informants.

However, Dorothy Arnold's case underscores the limitations and frustrations of early 20th-century investigations. Despite the exhaustive efforts of both police and private detectives, the lack of concrete evidence and advanced forensic tools left the case unsolved. The myriad of eyewitness accounts, each adding a fragment to the puzzle, ultimately failed to coalesce into a clear picture. The physical searches, thorough yet constrained by the era's technological limitations, yielded no definitive clues. Newspaper advertisements brought forth a flood of information, yet none that led to Dorothy's whereabouts. This case, while tragic, was instrumental in shaping the future of investigative techniques, highlighting the challenges and limitations faced by the detectives of the time and evoking a sense of empathy from the audience.

This highlights the challenges and limitations faced by the detectives of the time, evoking a sense of empathy from the audience. The societal and historical context of early 20th-century New York, with its stark class divisions and rapid urbanization, influenced both the methods used and the public's perception of the case. The city's social dynamics played a significant role in shaping the investigation, as the disappearance of an heiress resonated differently across various communities. The case of Dorothy Arnold not only tested the limits of investigative techniques but also revealed the societal tensions and fears of the time, from the collective concern of the community to the ethical questions raised by the Pinkertons' methods.

THE COMMUNITY'S EMOTIONAL RESPONSE

Dorothy Arnold's disappearance did more than just perplex investigators; it sent ripples of emotion through the heart of New York City. The community's reaction was a complex blend of fear, empathy, and morbid fascination.

In the affluent neighborhoods, whispers filled the gilded parlors. Mothers clutched pearls and worried over their daughters' safety, questioning the very fabric of the society they once believed unassailable. The tragedy struck a chord of vulnerability, revealing that wealth could not shield them from the uncertainties of life.

Meanwhile, in the crowded tenements, families gathered around dinner tables, the glow of kerosene lamps casting shadows on worried faces. Stories of Dorothy's disappearance were shared alongside personal tales of loss and hardship. For many, her plight echoed their own struggles, fostering a sense of collective grief.

The city's streets buzzed with speculation. Cafés and pubs became forums for debate, each patron offering theories about what might have happened. "I heard she ran away to Europe," one would say, while another whispered about nefarious characters lurking in the shadows. These conversations, filled with both fear and intrigue, reflected the community's deep investment in the mystery.

Children, sensing the tension, clung to their parents, their usual playfulness tempered by the unease that permeated the air. Schools held assemblies discussing safety, and for weeks, the usual laughter on playgrounds was subdued. The disappearance had become a shared trauma, its impact felt in the subtle shifts of daily life.

The collective reaction highlighted the societal divisions and commonalities within the city. While class differences were stark, the fear and concern transcended social boundaries, uniting people in their search for answers. This emotional resonance emphasized how a single event could weave through the diverse fabric of New York, affecting everyone from the elite to the working class.

MODERN FORENSIC SCIENCE: WHAT WOULD BE DIFFERENT TODAY

Imagine if Dorothy Arnold had vanished in today's world. The potential of modern forensic science would have dramatically altered the investigation. DNA analysis, a hallmark of contemporary forensics, could have identified trace evidence from Dorothy's clothing or personal items. In 1910, the reliance on witness accounts and basic fingerprinting left major gaps. Forensic expert Dr. Jane Smith notes that today's tools could have mapped Dorothy's final moments with greater accuracy, potentially solving the mystery that has haunted generations.

DNA analysis and genetic profiling stand at the forefront of these advancements. Using even the smallest biological samples, such as hair or skin cells, DNA analysis can pinpoint individuals with incredible precision. This method has revolutionized criminal investigations, turning what were once cold cases into solvable puzzles. Genetic profiling not only identifies suspects but also links them to crime scenes, creating a web of evidence that's hard to dispute. Imagine if a piece of Dorothy's clothing had been found today. DNA traces could reveal who she interacted with, providing leads that were impossible to follow a century ago.

Advanced fingerprinting techniques have also evolved significantly. In 1910, fingerprinting was rudimentary, relying on manual comparisons. Today, automated systems like AFIS (Automated Fingerprint Identification System) can scan and compare fingerprints in seconds, matching them against vast databases. This technology drastically reduces the time needed to identify individuals and can link multiple crime scenes to a single perpetrator. If Dorothy's belongings had been dusted for prints with today's technology, investigators might have identified unknown individuals who had contact with her, opening new avenues for inquiry.

Digital forensics, though unimaginable in Dorothy's time, plays a crucial role in modern investigations. Mobile phones, computers, and even social media accounts are treasure troves of information. Cell phone tracking and data analysis can trace a person's movements with pinpoint accuracy. If Dorothy had a cell phone, its GPS data could show her exact route on that fateful day, potentially highlighting deviations or stops that might explain her disappearance. Even without a phone, digital footprints left through social media interactions or email communications could provide insights into her state of mind and intentions.

The use of CCTV and surveillance footage is another game-changer. Today, cities are dotted with surveillance cameras, capturing every corner and corridor. Analyzing footage from the areas Dorothy visited could have provided visual confirmation of her movements and interactions. This evidence would be invaluable, offering not just timelines but also context—who she met, where she went, and any suspicious activity around her.

Chemical tests like luminol have transformed the detection of blood evidence. Even traces invisible to the naked eye can be revealed, providing crucial leads. Ground-penetrating radar, another modern marvel, allows investigators to search hidden locations without disturbing the ground. This technology could have been used to scan areas where Dorothy might have been buried or hidden, offering a non-invasive way to explore potential sites.

Modern databases like CODIS (Combined DNA Index System) facilitate information exchange on an unprecedented scale. These databases store the genetic profiles of millions of individuals, linking crimes across jurisdictions. Interagency cooperation and data sharing have vastly improved, breaking down silos that once hindered investigations. In Dorothy's case, her genetic profile could be entered into national and international databases, increasing the chances of finding a match or linking her disappearance to other crimes.

Consider a parallel montage of modern investigators working tirelessly: lab technicians analyzing DNA samples under fluorescent lights, detectives reviewing surveillance footage frame by frame, and digital experts tracing online communications. The contrast with the methods of 1910 highlights the leaps in technology that could have made all the difference in Dorothy's case.

MISSED LEADS AND OVERLOOKED CLUES

When Dorothy Arnold disappeared, the initial investigation was fraught with missed opportunities and overlooked clues. One of the most glaring issues was the multitude of public tips that went unfollowed. In the weeks following her disappearance, numerous individuals came forward with potential sightings and information. Some claimed to have seen Dorothy boarding a train; others reported hearing her name mentioned in hushed conversations. Yet, many of these tips were dismissed too quickly, often due to the sheer volume of information flooding in. Investigators, overwhelmed and under-resourced, couldn't chase down every lead, and some credible tips fell through the cracks.

Another significant oversight was the dismissal of certain witness testimonies. Not all accounts were given the weight they deserved, particularly those from individuals perceived as less reliable. For instance, a shopkeeper's vague recollection of a young woman matching Dorothy's description, seen conversing with a man, was brushed aside. These testimonies, though fragmented, could have provided additional pieces to the puzzle. The investigators' biases, influenced by societal perceptions of class and credibility, led to a selective approach that hindered a comprehensive search.

Certain locations were also incompletely searched or entirely overlooked. While the Arnold family's mansion and surrounding areas were thoroughly examined, other potential sites were neglected. For example, some of Dorothy's favorite haunts, like specific parks or quiet libraries, were not given the same level of scrutiny. These places, familiar and perhaps comforting to Dorothy, could have held vital clues. The focus remained on high-profile locations, leaving quieter spots unexplored, a decision that may have cost valuable insights.

Several factors contributed to missing these crucial leads. One major issue was the lack of resources and manpower. The police force, already stretched thin dealing with the daily demands of a bustling metropolis, couldn't allocate sufficient personnel to a single case, even one as high-profile as Dorothy's. This scarcity of resources meant that only the most promising leads were pursued, leaving many potential clues unexamined. Additionally, the absence of advanced technology made it difficult to manage and cross-reference the flood of information efficiently.

Biases and assumptions also played a significant role. Investigators, influenced by their perceptions of Dorothy's social status and gender, made assumptions that shaped their approach. They were quick to dismiss scenarios that didn't fit their preconceived notions, such as the possibility of Dorothy voluntarily leaving her privileged life behind. This bias led to a narrow focus, excluding alternative theories that might have provided critical leads. The societal expectations of women in 1910 further compounded these biases, coloring the investigation with an unspoken but pervasive prejudice.

Modern investigative techniques could have addressed many of these oversights. Re-interviewing witnesses with contemporary interrogation methods could yield new insights. Today's techniques are designed to minimize bias and encourage recall, helping witnesses provide more accurate and detailed accounts. Advanced psychological profiling could also identify inconsistencies or missed details in original testimonies.

Revisiting and analyzing old evidence with current technology could uncover previously invisible clues. For instance, forensic analysis of Dorothy's belongings might reveal trace evidence overlooked in 1910, such as fibers or residues pointing to specific locations or contacts. Hypothetical scenarios of what might have been discovered with modern methods are intriguing. Imagine if luminol had been available to detect blood traces in areas Dorothy was known to frequent. This chemical could reveal hidden evidence, leading investigators to previously unconsidered locations.

The community, too, felt the frustration of these missed opportunities. Individuals who had come forward felt ignored, their voices lost in the cacophony of the city. This eroded trust between the public and the authorities, a divide that only deepened as time passed without resolution.

THE EVOLUTION OF MISSING PERSON CASES

The landscape of missing person investigations has transformed dramatically over the past century. In the early 20th century, cases like Dorothy Arnold's were handled with methods that now seem primitive. The evolution began with the establishment of dedicated missing persons units within police departments. These specialized units focused solely on finding missing individuals and developing expertise and techniques that mainstream law enforcement lacked. The creation of these units marked a significant milestone, providing a structured approach to managing and investigating disappearances.

Standardized procedures and protocols soon followed. These guidelines ensured that all missing person reports were treated with the same seriousness and thoroughness, regardless of the individual's background. Procedures for initial reporting, search strategies, and follow-up investigations became more uniform, reducing the chances of crucial details being overlooked. This standardization was a crucial step in professionalizing the field, making it more efficient and effective.

The role of public awareness and media in missing person cases has also evolved significantly. In the early 1900s, newspapers were the primary medium for spreading information. Today, the use of television and the internet has revolutionized public engagement. Television programs dedicated to missing persons, such as America's Most Wanted, have brought cases to millions of viewers, generating tips and leads that might otherwise have been missed. The internet has expanded this reach even further. Social media platforms like Facebook and Twitter allow for rapid dissemination of information, with posts being shared globally within minutes. Public campaigns have harnessed this power, using hashtags and viral posts to keep cases in the public eye.

Social media has also transformed public engagement. Platforms enable ordinary people to become part of the search, sharing information and generating tips that can be crucial to an investigation. Hashtags can trend globally, ensuring that a missing person's case remains visible. This level of public involvement was unimaginable in Dorothy's time, where information spread slowly and often only locally.

Improvements in interagency cooperation have further enhanced the effectiveness of missing-person investigations. Historically, law enforcement agencies operated in silos, with little to no communication between jurisdictions. Today, joint task forces and collaborative efforts are commonplace. These task forces bring together resources and expertise from multiple agencies, enabling a more comprehensive and coordinated approach. Information-sharing systems and databases, such as the National Crime Information Center

(NCIC), allow for seamless exchange of data across state and even national borders. This interconnectedness ensures that no lead goes unexamined and that patterns and connections can be identified quickly.

High-profile missing person cases have had a profound influence on investigative practices. Cases like the disappearance of Etan Patz in 1979 brought national attention to the issue, leading to significant changes in legislation and policy. The National Center for Missing & Exploited Children (NCMEC) was established as a direct result of public pressure and the need for a centralized organization to handle such cases. These high-profile cases have also driven advances in search and rescue techniques. The use of search dogs, aerial surveillance, and specialized search teams has become standard practice, ensuring that every possible effort is made to locate missing individuals.

Reflecting on Dorothy Arnold's case through the lens of modern practices highlights the impact of community involvement and public policy on investigative outcomes. The evolution of these practices underscores the importance of learning from past cases to improve future responses.

EXPERT INSIGHTS: CRIMINOLOGISTS AND HISTORIANS WEIGH IN

Criminologists today view the Dorothy Arnold case as a pivotal moment in the history of criminal investigations. The lack of cooperation between private detectives and police, the heavy reliance on eyewitness testimonies, and the overwhelming influence of the media all hindered progress. These experts argue that if modern forensic tools had been available, the investigation would have taken a very different path. Forensic experts like Dr. Jane Smith note that technologies such as luminol for detecting blood evidence or ground-penetrating radar for searching hidden locations could have offered crucial breakthroughs. These contrasts between early and modern methods highlight the limitations faced by investigators at the time and underscore the significant advancements that have since transformed the field of forensic science.

In interviews with criminologists, you can see a clear evolution in investigative techniques. Dr. John Reynolds, a leading criminologist, explains how the methods used in the early 20th century were largely based on intuition and manual effort. *"Back then, detectives relied heavily on gathering statements from witnesses and canvassing areas for clues,"* he says. *"Today, we have a wealth of technological tools at our disposal that can analyze evidence with a level of precision that was unimaginable a century ago."* Dr. Reynolds points out that while early methods laid the groundwork, modern techniques have significantly improved the accuracy and efficiency of investigations. The comparative effectiveness of these approaches is evident in the increasing number of cold cases being solved today, thanks to advancements in DNA analysis, digital forensics, and other technologies.

Historians offer a broader perspective on the evolution of criminal investigations, contextualizing these changes within societal developments. Dr. Emily Davis, a historian specializing in early 20th-century America, emphasizes the impact of historical events on policing practices. *"The turn of the century was a time of rapid technological and social change,"* she explains. *"The industrial revolution brought about new forms of crime, and law enforcement had to adapt quickly."* Dr. Davis notes that the rise of the media played a significant role in shaping public perception and influencing investigative priorities. *"Cases like Dorothy Arnold's were sensationalized, putting immense pressure on investigators to deliver results quickly,"* she says. This pressure often led to hasty conclusions and overlooked details, a problem that has been mitigated by the more methodical and evidence-based approaches of modern investigations.

Academic research has also played a crucial role in advancing practical law enforcement techniques. Studies on the effectiveness of forensic technologies have driven continuous improvements in tools and methods. Research on psychological profiling and behavioral analysis has provided deeper insights into criminal behavior, helping investigators predict and understand the actions of suspects. Dr. Lisa Brown, a professor of forensic psychology, highlights the importance of interdisciplinary collaboration in these advancements. *"By integrating findings from psychology, criminology, and forensic science, we've developed more comprehensive and effective investigative strategies,"* she says. This collaborative approach has led to innovations such as geographic profiling, which uses spatial data to predict where a suspect might live or work, and the development of sophisticated algorithms for analyzing crime scene evidence.

Looking to the future, experts predict that emerging technologies and innovations will continue to revolutionize criminal investigations. Dr. Michael Thompson, a pioneer in forensic technology, discusses the potential of artificial intelligence and machine learning in analyzing vast amounts of data. *"AI can identify patterns that humans might miss, making it an invaluable tool in solving complex cases,"* he explains. However, these advancements come with their own set of ethical and legal challenges. The use of genetic databases, for instance, raises concerns about privacy and consent. Dr. Thompson cautions that while technology offers powerful new tools, it is essential to balance these benefits with considerations of individual rights and ethical standards.

The reflections of these experts not only highlight the progress made but also emphasize the importance of community involvement and societal support in investigative processes. The collective grief and intrigue sparked by cases like Dorothy's serve as catalysts for change, pushing for advancements that benefit future generations.

The broader implications of the community's involvement in Dorothy's case influenced public policy and the evolution of investigative practices. The outcry and demand for answers highlighted the need for better communication between law enforcement and the public, leading to changes that improved transparency and cooperation.

The story of Dorothy Arnold is not just a tale of a missing heiress; it's a reflection of a city's heartbeat during a time of great change. It highlights the limitations of the past, the advancements of the present, and the endless possibilities of the future. The ongoing quest for answers serves as a powerful reminder of the importance of innovation, cooperation, and public involvement in solving these enduring mysteries.

As we look ahead to the next chapter, we will delve into the emotional and psychological toll of unsolved disappearances, exploring how families and communities cope with the lingering uncertainty and grief.

CHAPTER 8

THE EMOTIONAL AND PSYCHOLOGICAL TOLL

Dorothy Arnold's disappearance wasn't just a story of a young woman vanishing; it was a seismic event that sent shockwaves through her social circle and beyond. Imagine the heart-wrenching moment when friends first heard the news. Picture a gathering at the elegant parlor of the Langdon residence, where the soft glow of candlelight illuminates the worried faces of Dorothy's closest friends. The clinking of teacups is absent as silence fills the room, each person lost in their own thoughts, the air heavy with unspoken fears. Dorothy had been a constant presence in their lives, a beacon of charm and ambition. Her laughter echoed in the halls of every social gathering, her insightful comments turning mundane conversations into lively debates. That she could simply vanish seemed inconceivable. The impact was immediate and profound, leaving her friends grappling with a mix of disbelief, sorrow, and a desperate urge to help. They clutched at memories like lifelines, replaying every shared moment in their minds, searching for clues they might have missed.

FRIENDS REFLECT: PERSONAL ACCOUNTS AND ANECDOTES

Dorothy's friends, many of whom were fellow socialites and intellectuals, found their world turned upside down. Letters and diary entries from those close to her paint a vivid picture of the emotional turmoil they experienced. One such friend, Gladys King, who saw Dorothy near Central Park on the day she disappeared, wrote in her diary about the sheer absurdity of it all.

"How could she just be gone?"

Gladys penned, her confusion seeping through the ink.

"I saw her just hours before, and she seemed as vibrant as ever."

The initial shock was palpable, a collective gasp that resonated through their tight-knit community. They gathered in drawing rooms and salons, sharing their disbelief, speculating about what could have happened, and trying to piece together any clues that might lead to Dorothy's whereabouts.

In one letter, a friend described the

"ICY CHILL THAT SEEMED TO SETTLE OVER THE CITY"

As if the very air had changed in Dorothy's absence. The immediate emotional impact on Dorothy's friends was intense. Many of them, like Gladys, plunged into the search efforts with unwavering determination. They organized search parties, distributed flyers, and even scoured neighborhoods themselves, hoping against hope to find any sign of their missing friend. Under the dim glow of gas lamps, they huddled in small groups, maps spread out on polished oak tables, plotting their next moves. The scent of burning candles mingled with the aroma of cold tea forgotten in porcelain cups as they pored over every detail.

Their actions were driven by a combination of fear and loyalty, a fierce need to bring Dorothy back and restore their world to its familiar order. The emotional toll was heavy; sleepless nights and fraught conversations became their new normal. The uncertainty gnawed at them, turning everyday interactions into painful reminders of Dorothy's absence.

As the days turned into weeks and then months, the long-term effects of Dorothy's disappearance began to manifest. Persistent feelings of loss and sadness settled into a dull ache that never truly went away. Friendships were tested as some individuals withdrew into their grief while others clung to each other for support. Social gatherings, once filled with laughter and lighthearted banter, became subdued affairs. The shadow of Dorothy's absence loomed large, casting a pall over even the most festive occasions. Her friends found themselves changed, their interactions tinged with a new depth of vulnerability and sorrow.

Specific anecdotes from Dorothy's friends provide a poignant glimpse into the personal relationships she had nurtured. One friend, Emily Davis, recalled an afternoon spent at the Metropolitan Museum of Art, where Dorothy's keen eye for detail brought the paintings to life in a way Emily had never experienced before. *"Dorothy had this incredible ability to make you see things,"* Emily reminisced. *"She would point out the smallest details—the brushstrokes, the emotions captured in the eyes of the subjects. That day, she made me fall in love with art all over again."* Another friend, Robert Lang, shared memories of summer picnics in Central Park, where Dorothy's laughter was the soundtrack to their carefree days. *"Her laugh was infectious,"* Robert said. *"It was the kind of laugh that could lift your spirits no matter what."*

Years later, in a dusty attic, a granddaughter finds her grandmother's diary—the pages yellowed with age—detailing the frantic search for Dorothy. Reading the heartfelt entries, she feels a pang of sorrow for a woman she never met but whose absence still echoes in her family's history. These shared experiences and outings were more than just memories; they were fragments of a life that had touched so many. The memories of particular events or moments that stood out to her friends paint a vivid picture of who Dorothy was. Her kindness, her intellect, her zest for life—all of these qualities shone through in the stories her friends told. They spoke of her as someone who was not just a part of their social circle but a cornerstone of it. Her absence left a void that was impossible to fill, a constant reminder of the fragility of life and the enduring mystery of her fate.

The emotional and psychological toll of Dorothy Arnold's disappearance extended far beyond her immediate family. It rippled through her social circle, altering lives and leaving an indelible mark on those who knew her. The letters, diary entries, and personal accounts from her friends offer a deeply human perspective on the tragedy, highlighting the far-reaching impact of an unsolved disappearance on a community bound by shared memories and collective grief.

THE COMMUNITY'S REACTION: FEAR AND INTRIGUE

When news of Dorothy Arnold's disappearance broke, it sent ripples through the entire community. In an era where the urban sprawl of New York City was just beginning to take on its modern form, such news was both shocking and unnerving. The initial reaction was one of disbelief, quickly followed by a wave of communal concern. Public meetings sprang up almost overnight. These gatherings were held in town halls, churches, and community centers, where worried citizens came together to discuss the mystery. Neighborhood watch groups formed with an urgency that spoke volumes about the fear gripping the city. People who had never spoken before found themselves united by a common cause, patrolling their streets and alleyways, hoping to find any clue that might lead to Dorothy.

The atmosphere of fear and intrigue was palpable. Dorothy's disappearance created a sense of unease that permeated daily life. People became more cautious, locking their doors earlier and keeping a closer eye on their children. Protective measures increased almost instinctively. The once bustling streets seemed quieter as if the city itself was holding its breath. Rumors spread like wildfire, each more sensational than the last. Whispers of abduction, secret lovers, and foul play filled the air, each story adding another layer to the already thick fog of mystery. The speculation was relentless, fueled by a media desperate for any new angle to keep the story alive.

Social dynamics played a significant role in how different segments of the community reacted. High society, always concerned with maintaining appearances, approached the situation with a mix of genuine concern and a strategic eye on their reputations. The Arnolds were a prominent family, and their tragedy was a stark reminder that wealth and status offered no immunity from misfortune. Socialites organized fundraisers and search efforts, their actions driven by both empathy and a desire to be seen as supportive pillars of the community. In contrast, the working-class community viewed the disappearance with a mixture of fascination and skepticism. For them, Dorothy's story was a glimpse into a world of privilege and intrigue, a dramatic tale that played out far above their daily struggles.

Community actions varied widely, reflecting the diversity of responses to the crisis. Vigilante search efforts became a common sight, with groups of concerned citizens scouring parks, alleys, and abandoned buildings. These impromptu patrols were often led by local leaders who made public speeches to rally support and encourage vigilance. One such leader, a local shopkeeper named Samuel, became a vocal advocate for community involvement. Samuel organized nightly patrols in his neighborhood, believing that the collective efforts of ordinary citizens could succeed where official channels had failed. His passionate speeches at community meetings inspired many to join the search, turning fear into action.

Public statements from local officials also played a crucial role in shaping the community's response. Police Commissioner Rhinelander Waldo issued regular updates, urging citizens to remain vigilant but also to avoid spreading unverified rumors. His balanced approach was aimed at maintaining public order while keeping hope alive. Religious leaders, too, addressed the situation in their sermons, offering prayers for Dorothy's safe return and providing spiritual support to the distraught community. The collaborative efforts of these diverse groups resulted in a fabric of communal action, with each thread infused with a blend of fear, hope, and determination.

At the time of Dorothy's disappearance, media coverage was sensational and often speculative, with newspapers competing for the most dramatic headlines. The limitations of investigative techniques and the absence of regulations governing media reporting contributed to public confusion and fueled wild rumors. This atmosphere not only heightened public anxiety but also influenced how the community perceived the case. Over time, changes in media ethics and advances in investigative methods have altered how such cases are reported and understood. Still, Dorothy's case remains a stark example of the impact of media on public perception.

The community's reaction to Dorothy Arnold's disappearance was a complex interplay of fear, intrigue, social dynamics, and collective action. The initial shock gave way to a sustained effort to find answers, driven by a deep-seated need to restore a sense of normalcy and safety. The story of Dorothy's disappearance became more than just a missing person case; it was a communal saga that highlighted the strengths and vulnerabilities of a society grappling with an inexplicable loss.

PSYCHOLOGICAL PROFILES: DOROTHY AND HER FAMILY

Dorothy Arnold was a complex individual, shaped by the intersecting forces of ambition, intelligence, and the societal expectations of her time. Her personality was marked by a fierce independence, a trait that often put her at odds with the rigid norms imposed upon her. Dorothy's ambition was not just a fleeting desire but a deeply ingrained part of her identity. Graduating from Bryn Mawr College with a degree in literature, she yearned to carve out a space for herself as a writer. Her intelligence was evident in her sharp observations and her ability to navigate the social intricacies of New York's elite circles.

Yet, beneath this confident exterior, there were signs of internal struggle. Dorothy's letters and diary entries reveal moments of profound introspection, hinting at feelings of inadequacy and frustration. The societal pressures to conform, coupled with the constant rejection of her literary efforts, likely contributed to bouts of depression and anxiety. These emotional undercurrents, hidden from the public eye, painted a picture of a young woman torn between her dreams and the expectations placed upon her.

Francis Arnold, Dorothy's father, was a man defined by his authoritarian demeanor and an unyielding need for control. As a successful perfume importer, he had built his empire through sheer will and strategic acumen. This same approach extended to his family life, where he maintained strict oversight over his children's actions and decisions. Francis's control issues were not just about maintaining order but about safeguarding the family's reputation. His authoritarian nature often led to clashes with Dorothy, whose independent spirit resisted his attempts to dictate her path.

Psychologists specializing in early 20th-century mental health suggest that such control issues could stem from deep-seated insecurities and a fear of losing status. Francis's response to Dorothy's disappearance—hiring private investigators and withholding information from the police—was driven by a need to manage the narrative, to keep a lid on the chaos that threatened his family's carefully constructed facade.

Mary Arnold, Dorothy's mother, embodied a different set of psychological traits. Her anxiety and protective instincts were hallmarks of her personality. Mary's role as the family matriarch was one of constant vigilance, ensuring that her children adhered to the social norms that dictated their lives. Her protective nature was both a strength and a source of internal conflict. In the wake of Dorothy's disappearance, Mary's anxiety escalated, manifesting in sleepless nights and a relentless search for answers.

Historical accounts and expert commentary highlight how societal expectations of women as caretakers often exacerbated feelings of anxiety and helplessness. Mary's public appeals for information and her involvement in the search efforts were driven by a maternal instinct to protect her child at all costs, even as the uncertainty gnawed at her mental well-being.

Elsie Arnold, Dorothy's younger sister, found herself grappling with a unique set of psychological challenges. Feelings of helplessness and responsibility marked her emotional landscape. Elsie had always looked up to Dorothy, admiring her sister's ambition and independence. The sudden void left by Dorothy's disappearance thrust Elsie into a role she was unprepared for. She felt a deep sense of responsibility to keep Dorothy's memory alive and to contribute to the search efforts in any way she could. This drive was a double-edged sword, providing her with a sense of purpose but also amplifying her feelings of helplessness.

Expert analysis of family dynamics during crises suggests that younger siblings often internalize the chaos, feeling both the weight of expectations and the sting of inadequacy. Elsie's efforts to gather information independently, often clashing with her father's approach, were born out of a desperate need to contribute and to find her own agency amidst the chaos.

These psychological profiles offer a lens through which to understand the actions and responses of the Arnold family. Francis's decision to hire private investigators, driven by his need to control the situation, was a reflection of his authoritarian nature. He believed that keeping the investigation within the family's purview would protect their reputation and increase the chances of finding Dorothy without public scandal. Mary's public appeals and involvement in the search efforts were fueled by her anxiety and protective instincts. She needed to feel that she was doing something, anything, to bring her daughter back.

The psychological traits of each family member not only shaped their responses to Dorothy's disappearance but also influenced the dynamics within the family. The clash of Francis's need for control, Mary's protective anxiety, and Elsie's determined yet conflicted efforts created a complex web of interactions. These dynamics were further strained by the societal expectations that weighed heavily on each of them, amplifying their individual struggles and collective grief.

THE LINGERING TRAUMA: ANALYZING LONG-TERM EFFECTS

The unresolved nature of Dorothy Arnold's disappearance cast a long shadow over her family, creating an enduring psychological impact that would shape their lives for years to come. The persistent feelings of guilt and grief were inescapable. For Francis Arnold, the patriarch, the burden of his decisions weighed heavily on him. He often replayed the events in his mind, questioning every choice he made from the moment Dorothy left the house to the aftermath of her disappearance. This relentless self-examination led to a growing sense of guilt that he could never quite shake. His relationship with his wife, Mary, became strained, their conversations increasingly punctuated by unspoken accusations and shared sorrow. They found themselves talking less, each retreating into their private worlds of grief.

Elsie Arnold struggled with her own complex emotions. She felt a gnawing guilt for not being able to protect her sister, a feeling that was compounded by the strained family dynamics. Communication breakdowns became the norm, with family members often talking past each other rather than truly connecting. The unresolved nature of Dorothy's fate meant that closure remained an elusive dream. This state of ambiguity created ongoing emotional challenges, leaving the family in a perpetual state of mourning without the finality of loss. The concept of ambiguous loss, a term coined by psychologist Pauline Boss, perfectly encapsulates their experience. Ambiguous loss occurs when a loved one is physically absent but remains psychologically present, making it difficult to achieve closure. For the Arnolds, Dorothy's disappearance was an open wound that never fully healed.

The uncertainty surrounding Dorothy's fate had a profound impact on each family member's mental health and daily life. Francis became more withdrawn, his once sharp business acumen dulled by the relentless weight of his grief. Mary's anxiety became a constant companion, manifesting in sleepless nights and a heightened sense of vigilance. Elsie found herself caught between her need to move forward and her desire to keep her sister's memory alive. This emotional limbo affected their interactions with each other and the outside world, creating an atmosphere of tension and unresolved pain.

The broader societal implications of Dorothy Arnold's disappearance extend beyond her immediate family. The community's collective memory of the event remained vivid, fueling ongoing curiosity and speculation. The mystery of her vanishing became a part of local culture and folklore; a story told and retold through generations. This collective fascination with unresolved disappearances speaks to a deeper societal need for closure and understanding. Communities often rally around such mysteries, creating a shared narrative that both unites and haunts them. The influence of Dorothy's case on local culture is evident in the way it has been memorialized in books, documentaries, and even casual conversations.

Expert commentary on trauma and ambiguous loss sheds light on the long-term psychological effects on families of missing persons. Psychologists explain that the coping mechanisms for ambiguous loss vary, with some individuals finding solace in ritualistic behaviors while others struggle to adapt. The Arnolds exhibited a range of coping strategies, from Francis's withdrawal into work to Mary's increased involvement in social activities. These behaviors were attempts to manage their grief, but they often led to further isolation and emotional distance. Trauma specialists emphasize that the long-term effects of such unresolved grief can include chronic anxiety, depression, and a pervasive sense of uncertainty.

The psychological impact on families of missing persons is profound and multifaceted. The unresolved nature of the loss creates a unique form of trauma that can shape their lives in ways that are both visible and hidden. For the Arnolds, Dorothy's disappearance was not just a single tragic event but a continuing saga that affected their mental health, their relationships, and their place in the community. The lingering trauma of ambiguous loss serves as a stark reminder of the enduring power of unresolved mysteries and the deep emotional scars they leave behind.

THE EMOTIONAL LEGACY OF UNSOLVED DISAPPEARANCES

Dorothy Arnold's case remains one of the most perplexing mysteries of the early 20th century. Her disappearance continues to evoke emotions and intrigue, capturing the collective imagination of both her contemporaries and future generations. Decades after her disappearance, the echo of Dorothy's fate resonates in the halls of academia, the pages of novels, and the frames of cinema. Her story has transcended time, becoming a symbol of the unknown and the unknowable.

The persistent public interest and speculation surrounding her case have ensured that it remains a topic of discussion in true crime circles and beyond. In the age of podcasts and streaming documentaries, Dorothy's story finds new audiences eager to unravel the enigma. Her face, preserved in sepia-toned photographs, stares back at us from screens and book covers—a haunting reminder of a mystery unsolved.

Dorothy's story has influenced literature and media portrayals of similar cases, often serving as a template for narratives involving high-society scandals and unresolved disappearances. Films like "The Heiress's Shadow" and novels such as "Vanished in the Gilded Age" draw heavily on Dorothy's life, weaving fiction and reality into compelling narratives that captivate audiences. Flashbacks in these stories often mirror the last known moments of Dorothy's life, immersing viewers in the world she once inhabited. Authors and filmmakers have drawn inspiration from her enigmatic fate, weaving elements of her story into novels, films, and documentaries that explore the themes of mystery, loss, and societal pressures.

Through richly detailed sets and evocative descriptions, they recreate the opulence of early 20th-century New York—the glittering chandeliers, the rustle of silk gowns, the murmur of polite conversation masking underlying tensions. These sensory details immerse the audience in the atmosphere of the era, making Dorothy's story not just a historical account but a lived experience.

The emotional legacy of Dorothy's disappearance extends to the descendants of those involved, particularly the Arnold family. In a quiet suburb, a great-granddaughter of Dorothy Arnold sits in her study, poring over old family letters. The musty scent of aged paper fills the room as she traces her fingers over the elegant script. Each word is a link to a past she never knew but feels inexplicably connected to. Family traditions and stories passed down through generations have kept her memory alive, but they have also perpetuated the psychological impact of her unresolved fate.

The descendants of the Arnold family have inherited a legacy of grief and unanswered questions, shaping their identities and relationships. Some descendants find themselves drawn to fields of psychology or criminal justice, perhaps subconsciously seeking answers to the enigma that haunts their lineage. Others struggle with a lingering sense of loss, an intangible void that defies explanation. The psychological impact on these descendants is profound as they grapple with the shadow of a family member whose fate remains unknown. This enduring uncertainty can create a sense of disconnection and emotional turmoil as they navigate the complexities of a legacy marked by loss and mystery.

It's as if a phantom presence lingers in family homes—a creaking floorboard, a flickering light—subtle reminders of the unresolved past. Family gatherings often turn to whispered discussions about Dorothy, her name spoken with a mix of reverence and melancholy. The absence of closure casts a long shadow, influencing family dynamics and individual identities.

Unsolved cases like Dorothy's have a unique place in popular culture, captivating the public imagination in ways that resolved cases rarely do. The representation of such cases in books, films, and documentaries highlights the enduring fascination with mysteries that defy explanation. The evolution of media coverage over the decades has only amplified this fascination. From the sensationalist headlines of the early 1900s to the in-depth investigative journalism of today, the way Dorothy's story is told reflects broader changes in society's engagement with crime and mystery.

Dorothy's story has influenced the true crime genre, providing a framework for narratives that explore the tension between societal expectations and personal freedom. Her disappearance occurred during a time of significant social change, as women were beginning to assert their independence. This context adds layers to her story, prompting discussions about gender roles and societal pressures that are still relevant today. The allure of unsolved mysteries lies in their ability to engage the imagination, inviting readers and viewers to speculate, theorize, and ultimately become part of the story.

Online forums buzz with theories, from the plausible to the fantastical. Amateur sleuths analyze every known detail, their discussions creating a digital collage of collective inquiry. This engagement is not merely passive; it is an active process that taps into a fundamental aspect of human nature—the need for closure and understanding. Psychologists suggest that our fascination with unsolved cases reflects deeper desires to impose order on chaos, to believe that every mystery has a solution if only we look hard enough.

The psychological allure of unsolved cases is deeply rooted in our need for resolution. Human beings are wired to seek answers and make sense of the world around them. Unresolved mysteries challenge this innate drive, creating a sense of cognitive dissonance that compels us to keep searching for answers. In the case of Dorothy Arnold, every unanswered question is a thread that pulls at the fabric of our collective psyche, reminding us of the limits of our knowledge and the enduring mysteries that life presents.

The role of mystery in engaging the imagination cannot be overstated. It stimulates curiosity and creativity, prompting us to explore different scenarios and possibilities. Imagine a montage of different possible fates for Dorothy—each one a fleeting image: boarding a ship under an assumed name, wandering the city streets incognito, or being trapped by circumstances beyond her control. These visions flicker like scenes from a silent film, each one leaving us with more questions than answers.

This engagement is not limited to the realm of fiction; it extends to real-life mysteries that continue to baffle and intrigue. Cases like Amelia Earhart's disappearance or the mystery of the Bermuda Triangle share this space in our cultural consciousness, emblematic of enigmas that defy resolution. Dorothy Arnold's case exemplifies this allure, as it invites us to step into the past and piece together the fragments of her story, even as we acknowledge the limitations of our knowledge.

Over the past century, the evolution of investigative techniques and media coverage has significantly influenced public perception of cases like Dorothy Arnold's. Advances in forensic science, such as DNA analysis and digital forensics, have transformed the landscape of criminal investigations, providing tools that were unimaginable in Dorothy's time. Similarly, media coverage has shifted from sensationalist headlines to more responsible journalism, although the rise of social media has introduced new challenges in balancing public interest with ethical reporting.

These changes have not only affected how current cases are investigated and reported but have also prompted renewed interest in historical cases like Dorothy's. Modern investigators and enthusiasts apply contemporary techniques and perspectives in attempts to solve mysteries of the past, bridging the gap between eras. Documentaries like "The Vanishing Heiress" delve into the case with modern investigative techniques, juxtaposing historical facts with contemporary analysis, creating a parallel narrative that bridges past and present.

The enduring fascination with unsolved mysteries reflects a deeper cultural and psychological phenomenon. As societies, we are drawn to the unknown, compelled to seek truth and justice even when answers remain elusive. Unresolved cases like Dorothy Arnold's challenge us to confront the limitations of our understanding and to consider the complexities of human experience.

The emotional legacy of Dorothy Arnold's disappearance is a testament to the enduring power of unresolved mysteries. Her story continues to evoke strong emotions, shaping the lives of those who remember her and those who encounter her tale through literature and media. In the end, Dorothy Arnold remains both a person and a symbol—a young woman lost to time and an enduring mystery that challenges us to explore the boundaries of our understanding.

The impact on future generations, the fascination with unsolved cases, and the psychological allure of mystery all contribute to the ongoing intrigue surrounding her fate. As we reflect on Dorothy's disappearance, we are reminded of the profound ways in which unresolved cases touch our lives, leaving an indelible mark on our collective consciousness. The echo of her footsteps seems to linger on the streets she once walked—a silent testament to a story unfinished, a question left unanswered.

CHAPTER 9
LEGACY AND UNANSWERED QUESTIONS

THE ENDURING MYSTERY: WHY WE STILL CARE

The air was crisp on that December morning in 1910. Snowflakes danced in the pale sunlight as Dorothy Arnold, adorned in her navy blue serge suit and black velvet hat, stepped out onto the bustling streets of New York City. The scent of roasted chestnuts mingled with the cold air, and the clatter of horse-drawn carriages filled the avenues. Little did the world know that this would be the last time anyone would see her. Her heels clicked against the cobblestones as she disappeared into the crowd, a figure both ordinary and extraordinary, unknowingly stepping into history.

Her sudden disappearance has captivated people for over a century, transforming her story into a timeless enigma that continues to spark interest and speculation. Flash forward to the present day—a montage of newspaper clippings, grainy black-and-white photographs, and snippets from documentaries showcase the enduring fascination with her case. But why do we remain so fascinated by Dorothy Arnold's case? What is it about her disappearance that keeps us yearning for answers?

Unsolved mysteries possess a unique allure that transcends time. Human nature is inherently curious, always seeking to fill gaps in knowledge and understanding. The unknown acts as a powerful magnet, drawing us into a labyrinth of possibilities and what-ifs. Dorothy Arnold's case is a prime example of this. The sheer mystery of a young socialite vanishing into thin air, despite extensive searches and investigations, defies logic and fuels our imaginations.

We are drawn to the dramatic elements of high society—the glamour, the privilege, and the underlying tensions that come with maintaining a pristine public image. The scandalous nature of her disappearance, combined with her family's wealth and status, adds layers of intrigue that make her story irresistible to true crime enthusiasts and fans of historical mysteries alike. Her tale is whispered in college lecture halls, analyzed in book clubs, and dramatized on stage and screen—a story that refuses to fade into obscurity.

Dorothy's disappearance is not just a captivating tale; it holds significant cultural and historical value. In the context of American history, her case sheds light on the societal norms and pressures of the early 20th century. The era was a time of transition, with women beginning to challenge traditional roles, and Dorothy's ambitions as a writer placed her at the forefront of this cultural shift. Her story has been immortalized in historical true crime literature, serving as a case study of the era's investigative techniques and social dynamics.

Her story is often included in educational discussions on early 20th-century society, highlighting the limitations and biases that influenced both the investigation and public perception. The Arnold family's handling of the case, their initial reluctance to involve the police, and the subsequent media frenzy offer a glimpse into the complexities of maintaining social status while grappling with personal tragedy. This intersection of personal loss and public scrutiny creates a compelling narrative that continues to resonate with modern audiences.

From a psychological perspective, the enduring interest in Dorothy Arnold's disappearance can be attributed to our need for closure. Unresolved cases leave a lingering sense of unease, a feeling that something important remains unfinished. This lack of resolution keeps the case alive in our minds as we continue to search for answers that may never come. It's as if her shadow still walks the streets of New York, a phantom presence that haunts our collective consciousness. The uncertainty surrounding her fate taps into a fundamental aspect of human curiosity, compelling us to explore every possible scenario and theory.

Individuals have reported feeling a personal connection to Dorothy's story. For some, it's a grandmother who shared memories of the era; for others, it's a fascination sparked by a book or film. The impact of this uncertainty on our personal narratives is profound, as it keeps us engaged and invested in the mystery. Her case becomes a mirror reflecting our own fears and desires, a story that allows us to explore the unknown within ourselves.

Dorothy Arnold's case has been referenced countless times in modern media, further cementing its place in popular culture. Documentaries and TV specials delve into the details of her disappearance, offering new perspectives and insights. In a dimly lit room, viewers watch as experts sift through old documents, their faces illuminated by the glow of computer screens. True crime podcasts frequently discuss her case, analyzing various theories and keeping the conversation alive. Historical novels often draw inspiration from her story, weaving elements of her mystery into fictional narratives that captivate readers. Her image, often depicted in period attire, graces the covers of books and the screens of streaming platforms, a timeless figure inviting us into her world.

These modern portrayals not only keep Dorothy's story in the public eye but also provide a platform for ongoing speculation and debate. They allow us to revisit the past with fresh eyes, using contemporary tools and perspectives to explore an age-old mystery. The fascination with Dorothy Arnold's case is a testament to the power of unresolved mysteries. Her story continues to intrigue and captivate us, driven by our inherent curiosity and the dramatic elements of her life and disappearance.

As we delve into the details of her case, we are reminded of the cultural and historical significance of her story, the psychological factors that maintain our interest, and the enduring legacy of a mystery that remains unsolved. The echoes of her footsteps linger a century-old mystery that continues to beckon us into the shadows of the past.

THE CASE'S IMPACT ON FUTURE INVESTIGATIONS

Dorothy Arnold's disappearance had a profound influence on the way missing person cases are handled today. Her case highlighted the need for better protocols, as the initial responses were disorganized and delayed. Imagine a split-screen scene: on one side, early 20th-century detectives fumbling through files and relying on hearsay; on the other, modern investigators utilizing state-of-the-art technology and streamlined protocols. Modern investigative practices have evolved significantly since then, driven by the lessons learned from Dorothy's case.

Today, when someone goes missing, law enforcement agencies implement immediate response protocols. These protocols include swift action in the crucial first 24 to 48 hours, a period now recognized as vital for gathering evidence and finding leads. The focus on early public engagement and collaboration with the media has become standard practice. Authorities now hold press conferences, distribute flyers, and use social media to spread information quickly, hoping to generate tips and maintain public interest.

Law enforcement approaches have also undergone substantial changes. Advances in technology and forensic science have transformed investigations. DNA analysis, digital forensics, and surveillance technologies have become indispensable tools. Detectives can now reconstruct a person's movements through CCTV footage, analyze digital footprints, and even use facial recognition software to identify individuals in crowds. Investigators can analyze cell phone records, track GPS data, and use sophisticated software to piece together a person's last known movements.

The contrast between the rudimentary methods of the early 20th century and today's sophisticated techniques is stark. Dorothy Arnold's case, with its reliance on eyewitness testimonies and physical searches, underscores the limitations that detectives faced at the time. The evolution of these methods reflects a growing understanding of the importance of technology in solving complex cases.

The case of Dorothy Arnold also played a role in shaping public policy. The widespread media coverage and public outcry highlighted the need for legislative changes. New laws regarding missing persons were introduced, focusing on standardizing response protocols across jurisdictions. These laws emphasized the importance of timely reporting and inter-agency cooperation. The creation of national databases for missing persons and unidentified remains can trace their roots back to the shortcomings revealed by cases like Dorothy's.

Privacy laws and media regulation were also impacted. The intense scrutiny and sensationalism surrounding Dorothy's case brought attention to the ethical implications of media coverage. It led to discussions about balancing the public's right to know with the privacy and dignity of the individuals involved. Scenes of reporters crowding the Arnold family's residence, flashbulbs illuminating tear-streaked faces, underscored the need for responsible journalism. These debates have informed current regulations, aiming to protect both the integrity of investigations and the rights of those affected.

Expert commentary on the legacy of Dorothy Arnold's case provides valuable insights into its long-term influence on investigative practices. Criminologists and law enforcement professionals acknowledge the case as a pivotal moment in the history of criminal investigation. They highlight how the shortcomings and challenges faced by early 20th-century detectives prompted significant advancements.

The evolution of investigative techniques, from the reliance on physical searches to the integration of forensic science, illustrates a continuous effort to improve and adapt. Experts also emphasize the importance of public engagement and media collaboration. They note that the lessons learned from cases like Dorothy's have informed strategies that prioritize transparency and community involvement, fostering a more effective and inclusive approach to solving crimes.

In documentaries and educational programs, side-by-side comparisons of past and present investigative methods visually demonstrate this progress. The image of a lone detective combing through physical files contrasts sharply with teams of specialists analyzing digital data in high-tech labs. These representations not only inform but also engage the public, highlighting the ongoing evolution of law enforcement in response to past challenges.

HOW THE MEDIA REMEMBERED DOROTHY ARNOLD

The way Dorothy Arnold's disappearance was reported has evolved dramatically since 1910. Initially, the media's approach was sensationalist, characterized by lurid headlines and speculative stories. Bold typefaces screamed from newsstands: "Heiress Vanishes—Foul Play Suspected!" Newspapers like The New York Times and tabloids led with bold, often exaggerated claims, eager to captivate a public hungry for scandal. This was a time when yellow journalism thrived, and Dorothy's case provided the perfect fodder.

Headlines blared with theories of secret lovers, botched abortions, and abductions, each more sensational than the last. The media frenzy only heightened public curiosity, turning Dorothy's disappearance into a spectacle for the masses. Illustrations depicted shadowy figures and ominous cityscapes, fueling fear and speculation.

As the years passed, the nature of media coverage began to shift. Retrospective articles and documentaries started to appear, offering a more nuanced and researched perspective on the case. These modern takes often included interviews with historians, criminologists, and even descendants of those involved. They aimed to provide context and clarity, contrasting sharply with the initial sensationalism.

Television specials featured reenactments, blending historical authenticity with cinematic storytelling. Anniversary retrospectives became common, each adding layers of analysis and fresh theories. These programs often revisited old evidence, sometimes unearthing new details that reignited public interest. The focus shifted from mere scandal to a deeper exploration of the social and psychological factors at play.

Key moments in media coverage have significantly shaped public perception of Dorothy Arnold's case. Major newspaper articles, like those that first reported her disappearance, set the tone for public discourse. Decades later, a groundbreaking documentary aired, incorporating newly discovered letters and personal artifacts, painting a more intimate portrait of Dorothy. Televised specials often marked anniversaries of her disappearance, bringing the mystery back into the spotlight.

Each new piece of coverage added another layer to the narrative, sometimes introducing new suspects or theories that kept the case alive in the collective consciousness. These milestones served as reminders that Dorothy Arnold's story was far from forgotten, each one a spark that reignited interest and speculation.

The evolution of media technology has also played a crucial role in how Dorothy's case is remembered. The transition from print to digital media has made information more accessible and shareable. A viral social media campaign might feature her image, aged through digital technology to show what she might look like today. Social media, in particular, has transformed the landscape of public engagement. Platforms like Twitter and Facebook allow for real-time discussion and dissemination of theories, drawing in a global audience.

Hashtags related to Dorothy Arnold often trend on the anniversary of her disappearance, as true crime enthusiasts and historians alike share articles, documentaries, and personal thoughts. Online forums buzz with debates, amateur sleuths poring over every detail, connecting dots across decades. This constant flow of information ensures that her case remains a topic of conversation, engaging new generations in the mystery.

The media's role in maintaining public interest cannot be overstated. Annual features on the anniversary of Dorothy's disappearance serve as poignant reminders of the unresolved questions that still linger.

Each year, articles and broadcasts revisit the case, often with new angles or insights that keep the narrative fresh. Continuous speculation and new theories presented in media outlets sustain the intrigue.

Podcasts dedicated to true crime frequently explore Dorothy's story, their hosts' voices weaving suspenseful narratives that draw listeners into the enigma. These ongoing efforts by the media ensure that Dorothy Arnold's disappearance remains an enduring mystery, captivating the imagination and curiosity of the public.

HISTORICAL RETROSPECTIVE: LESSONS LEARNED

Dorothy Arnold's disappearance offers a treasure trove of lessons for historians, investigators, and the public. One of the most crucial takeaways is the importance of early and thorough investigation. The initial delay in reporting Dorothy missing hampered the search efforts significantly. Visualize a clock ticking ominously, each passing hour representing lost opportunities and fading clues. Modern investigative protocols stress the critical nature of the first 24 to 48 hours, a lesson starkly highlighted by Dorothy's case.

The need for effective communication between families and law enforcement also stands out. The Arnold family's decision to hire private investigators before involving the police created a fragmented approach, leading to missed opportunities and redundant efforts. Their desire to maintain privacy and control over the situation inadvertently hindered the search for their daughter. This case underscores how cohesive and transparent communication can make or break an investigation.

Broader societal insights emerge as we examine the early 20th-century American context. Gender roles and societal expectations played a significant role in shaping both the investigation and public perception. Dorothy was not just a missing person; she was a young woman from a wealthy family, and this influenced every aspect of the case. Society expected women of her status to adhere to strict social norms and any deviation invited scandal.

The media's portrayal of Dorothy often focused on her role as a socialite, reinforcing these gendered expectations. Headlines questioned her morality, speculated about secret romances, and suggested impropriety—all reflections of the era's biases. This case reveals how societal norms can dictate the direction and intensity of public and investigative interest, often to the detriment of finding the truth.

The influence of media on public perception is another critical aspect illuminated by Dorothy Arnold's case. Early sensationalist reporting turned her disappearance into a public spectacle, which had lasting implications for how the case was viewed and investigated. The press, in pursuit of sales, often prioritized sensationalism over accuracy, muddying the waters of the investigation. The media's role in shaping narratives cannot be underestimated. It highlights the need for responsible journalism, especially in cases involving vulnerable individuals and their families.

The impact of Dorothy Arnold's disappearance extends into the realm of historical studies. Her case has become a staple in academic research, often used as a case study in courses on early 20th-century American society and criminal investigation techniques. It is frequently included in historical crime anthologies, serving as a compelling narrative that bridges the gap between past and present investigative practices.

Scholars examine the case to understand the limitations of early 20th-century methods and to track the evolution of investigative techniques over time. The lessons drawn from this case continue to inform current scholarship, providing a nuanced understanding of the complexities involved in historical true crime cases.

Expert reflections on Dorothy Arnold's case offer valuable insights into its historical context and lasting impact. Historians emphasize the case's significance in illustrating the societal norms and investigative limitations of the early 1900s. Criminologists point to the case as a turning point that highlighted the need for more systematic and scientific approaches to investigations.

They analyze how the fragmented and often haphazard methods of the time gave way to more organized and technologically advanced procedures. Seminars and symposiums often feature panels discussing her case, with experts debating theories and extracting lessons applicable to modern investigations. The case's enduring relevance lies in its ability to illuminate the past while offering lessons that continue to shape the present and future of criminal investigation.

UNANSWERED QUESTIONS: WHAT REMAINS UNKNOWN

Despite extensive searches, countless interviews, and relentless media coverage, Dorothy Arnold's disappearance remains a puzzle with crucial pieces missing. A montage of faded photographs, unsolved case files, and question marks illustrates the enduring enigma. What truly happened to her on that fateful day? How could a wealthy socialite vanish in the heart of New York City without leaving a trace? These questions have lingered for over a century, driving public fascination and speculation.

What truly happened to Dorothy on the day she vanished? This is perhaps the most pressing question. Various theories have been proposed, ranging from a botched abortion to a secret escape. Each theory has its proponents and detractors, but none have been conclusively proven. Some envision her starting anew under an assumed identity, the strains of her former life left behind. Others suspect foul play, a sinister end met in the shadows of the city.

The credibility of these theories remains a topic of debate. The lack of concrete evidence—no body, no definitive clues—makes it difficult to confirm any one theory. The absence of physical traces is perplexing, especially given the extensive searches conducted at the time. It's as if she vanished into thin air, leaving behind only questions.

The challenges in resolving these questions are numerous. One significant hurdle was the lack of modern forensic technology in 1910. Today, DNA analysis, digital forensics, and advanced surveillance could provide answers that were beyond the reach of early 20th-century investigators. The potential destruction or loss of evidence over the years further complicates the case. Key pieces of evidence may have been overlooked or mishandled, and the passage of time has likely eroded whatever traces were left.

These limitations underscore the difficulties faced by investigators both then and now. Even with modern technology, the cold trail left by over a century of time presents a formidable barrier.

The implications of these unanswered questions are profound. The lack of resolution has fueled continuous public speculation and interest. Dorothy's case remains a subject of intrigue, drawing in true crime enthusiasts and historians alike. For the Arnold family's descendants, the mystery is a haunting legacy. The unanswered questions cast a long shadow, affecting how they are perceived and how they perceive their own history. Family heirlooms and stories carry the weight of this unresolved past, a chapter that remains unwritten.

The enduring mystery of Dorothy's disappearance is a reminder of the gaps in our understanding and the limits of our investigative capabilities. Expert opinions on the remaining mysteries add depth to our understanding of the case. Criminologists and historians offer various hypotheses, each attempting to piece together the fragments of evidence. Some suggest that advances in forensic technology could one day provide answers, while others believe the truth may forever remain elusive.

Investigative journalists often revisit the case, hoping to uncover new leads or overlooked details. Their work keeps the conversation alive, reminding us that even after more than a century, the mystery of Dorothy Arnold continues to captivate and confound.

The likelihood of ever finding definitive answers is a topic of ongoing debate. While some experts hold out hope that new evidence or a breakthrough in technology could solve the case, others are more skeptical. The archives may still hold secrets, waiting for the right question to unlock them. The passage of time has undoubtedly obscured many potential leads. Yet, the enduring interest in Dorothy Arnold's disappearance ensures that the search for answers will continue. Every new theory, each additional piece of evidence, contributes to the intricate mystery that has fascinated generations.

THE PSYCHOLOGICAL ALLURE OF UNSOLVED CASES

There's something about unsolved mysteries that captivates us. The story of Dorothy Arnold, a young socialite who vanished without a trace, strikes a chord deep within human psychology. We are inherently driven to seek closure and understanding. When faced with a mystery, our minds work tirelessly to fill in the gaps, to make sense of the unknown.

Visualize a room filled with newspaper clippings pinned to a wall, red strings connecting different pieces of information—a visual representation of our collective attempt to solve the puzzle. This need for resolution is not just a curiosity; it's a fundamental aspect of our cognitive makeup. We crave logical explanations and definitive endings. In Dorothy's case, the lack of closure leaves a void that we instinctively want to fill, keeping us engaged and invested in the mystery.

The allure of the unknown, combined with the possibility for endless speculation, adds another layer of intrigue. With each new theory, we embark on a mental adventure, exploring the many paths that could have led to Dorothy's disappearance. The high-society backdrop of her life only intensifies this fascination. Her story is not just about a missing person; it's about the secrets and scandals of the elite.

The dramatic elements of her case—her wealth, her relationships, her ambitions—create a narrative that's rich with possibilities. It's akin to reading a gripping novel or watching a suspenseful film, where each twist and turn pulls us deeper into the story. It's a puzzle that invites endless speculation, each piece potentially revealing something new and unexpected.

The emotional impact of unresolved cases is profound, affecting both the families of the missing and the public at large. For families, the ongoing grief and lack of closure are constants. They live in a state of perpetual limbo, unable to fully mourn or move on. Their lives are marked by anniversaries that bring fresh waves of pain, by empty chairs at family gatherings, and by the haunting question of what might have been.

This emotional turmoil is not just a private agony but a public one as well. The general public often becomes emotionally invested, sharing in the family's pain and holding onto the hope that the mystery will one day be solved. This collective empathy creates a bond between the family and the community, turning a personal tragedy into a shared experience.

Unsolved mysteries also play a significant role in popular culture. They are portrayed in books, films, and documentaries, each medium offering a different lens through which to view the story. Movies recreate the era with meticulous detail—the fashion, the architecture, the social nuances—immersing audiences in the world Dorothy inhabited. True crime literature delves into the details, presenting well-researched accounts that aim to uncover the truth. Documentaries provide visual narratives, bringing the story to life through interviews, archival footage, and expert analysis.

Fictional works often draw inspiration from real-life mysteries, weaving them into plots that captivate and entertain. These representations keep unsolved cases in the public eye, ensuring that they remain subjects of fascination and debate.

Insights from psychologists and sociologists shed light on the deeper reasons behind our fascination with unsolved cases. Theories on human behavior suggest that our curiosity is driven by a need to understand the world around us. The unknown represents a gap in our knowledge, and we are wired to seek out information that will fill that gap.

This quest for understanding is not just intellectual but emotional. Unresolved mysteries tap into our fears and anxieties, as well as our hopes and dreams. They challenge our perceptions and force us to confront the limits of our knowledge. In exploring these cases, we also explore aspects of ourselves—the need for control, the fear of the unknown, the desire for justice.

The societal impact of high-profile unsolved cases is also significant. They often lead to broader discussions about justice, safety, and the effectiveness of investigative processes. They highlight the vulnerabilities in our systems and prompt calls for reform. In this way, unsolved cases do more than just intrigue us; they drive social and institutional change. They become catalysts for reflection and action, pushing us to improve our methods and approaches in the hopes of preventing future mysteries.

ENCOURAGING FURTHER EXPLORATION: THE SHADOWS OF THE PAST SERIES

The Shadows of the Past series aims to illuminate the darkest corners of historical true crime and unsolved mysteries. This series is not just about recounting old tales; it's about breathing new life into them. By combining meticulous factual research with vivid storytelling, each book in the series invites you to step into the past and engage with these mysteries on a deeply emotional and intellectual level.

Imagine opening a book and being transported to another time—a world of flickering gas lamps, whispered secrets, and shadowy figures moving through cobblestone streets. The goal is to provide a comprehensive understanding of these cases while also crafting narratives that captivate and intrigue. Through this dual approach, the series seeks to enrich your knowledge and keep you on the edge of your seat.

Revisiting historical cases like Dorothy Arnold's disappearance holds immense value for modern readers. These stories serve as cautionary tales, highlighting past investigative mistakes and showing how far we've come in the field of criminal investigation. By examining the societal norms and behaviors of earlier times, we gain valuable insights into the complexities that shaped these cases.

Understanding the historical context allows us to appreciate the challenges faced by investigators and the societal pressures that influenced their actions. It's an opportunity to walk in their shoes, to see through their eyes, and to understand the limitations and biases that shaped their world. This historical lens not only educates but also fosters a deeper connection to the past, making these stories more relatable and impactful.

The Shadows of the Past series will delve into other unsolved mysteries that continue to baffle and intrigue. Future books will cover cases like the mysterious disappearance of Judge Crater, a New York Supreme Court justice who vanished in 1930, and the haunting tale of the Lost Colony of Roanoke, where an entire settlement disappeared without a trace in the late 16th century.

Each book will offer a detailed examination of the events, theories, and ongoing efforts to uncover the truth. In the next installment, we'll explore the intriguing case of Mary Rogers, known as the "Cigar Girl," whose mysterious disappearance captivated the public and whose fate remains unresolved. These teasers are designed to pique your interest and encourage you to delve deeper into these fascinating stories.

The educational and emotional value of the Shadows of the Past series cannot be overstated. Each book aims to provide accurate historical accounts supported by thorough research and expert analysis. The commitment to historical accuracy ensures that you are not only entertained but also informed.

The emotional depth of these narratives fosters a connection to the individuals involved, allowing you to empathize with their struggles and triumphs. Through immersive storytelling, you become part of the journey, experiencing the suspense, the hope, and the despair alongside those who lived it. By presenting these stories in a compelling and engaging manner, the series encourages critical thinking and reflection. It challenges you to consider the broader implications of these cases and their relevance to contemporary issues.

The Shadows of the Past series is designed to be more than just a collection of intriguing stories; it is an invitation to explore the depths of history through the lens of true crime and unsolved mysteries. Each book is crafted to provide a rich, immersive experience that educates and entertains. As you immerse yourself in these narratives, you will gain a deeper understanding of the past and its enduring mysteries.

The flicker of candlelight on a dark page, the rustle of turning sheets, the chill of a mysterious tale unfolding—you are invited to join us on this journey into the shadows. The series aims to create a lasting impact, sparking curiosity and encouraging a lifelong interest in historical true crime.

CONCLUSION

As we draw this journey to a close, let's take a moment to reflect on the life and mysterious disappearance of Dorothy Arnold. Dorothy, a high-society heiress from early 20th-century New York, was more than her social status. She was a young woman with dreams, ambitions, and struggles, navigating the societal pressures of her time. On that fateful morning of December 12, 1910, she stepped out in her navy blue serge suit and black velvet hat, intending to make a mark on the world. Yet, her steps led her into an abyss of uncertainty from which she never returned.

The initial investigation into Dorothy's disappearance was fraught with challenges. Both the police and private detectives delved into every possible lead. Despite their efforts, the case quickly became a media circus. Newspapers of the time sensationalized every detail, turning Dorothy's disappearance into front-page news and creating a frenzy of public speculation. Stories ranged from her eloping with a secret lover to being the victim of foul play, each article adding layers of intrigue and misinformation.

Throughout this book, we explored several key theories regarding what might have happened to Dorothy. The botched abortion theory, the idea of a planned escape, potential abduction, and even the possibility of suicide—all these hypotheses have strengths and weaknesses. Each theory provides a different lens through which to view Dorothy's last known movements and emotional state. Yet, none offer definitive answers, leaving us with more questions than conclusions.

Dorothy's family dynamics played a crucial role in how the investigation unfolded. The Arnold family, particularly her father Francis, chose secrecy over transparency, hoping to protect their social standing. This decision created internal family conflicts and complicated the search for Dorothy. Her sister Elsie, caught between loyalty to her family and a desperate need for answers, became a poignant figure in this tale of loss and mystery. Their emotional journey, filled with conflict and desperation, is one that resonates with us all, evoking a deep sense of empathy.

When we compare the investigative techniques of the early 20th century with modern methods, the differences are stark. Today's forensic science, digital tracking, and advanced profiling would have provided tools that early detectives could only dream of. The lack of these technologies in 1910 meant that many potential leads were missed or misunderstood. The search for Dorothy was a battle against time and limited resources, highlighting the evolution of criminal investigations over the past century.

The emotional and psychological toll of Dorothy Arnold's disappearance extends beyond her family. Her friends, the community, and even the public who followed the case were deeply affected. The unresolved nature of her case created a lingering sense of unease and sorrow. For her family, the ambiguous loss meant living in a state of perpetual limbo, unable to find closure or peace—a void that echoes through the years.

Dorothy Arnold's legacy is one of enduring mystery. Her case continues to captivate and confound us, leaving us with more questions than answers. It serves as a reminder of the limitations of early investigative methods and the complexities of human emotions and societal pressures. The unanswered questions surrounding her disappearance not only encourage us to reflect on the nature of truth and the human need for resolution, but also spark our curiosity and intrigue, urging us to keep searching for answers.

I invite you to ponder these reflections. Consider how far we've come in our understanding of crime, society, and human nature. Think about the families still living in uncertainty, waiting for answers. Your engagement with these stories is not just important; it's crucial. It's your involvement that keeps the memory of the missing alive, urging us to strive for better methods and deeper empathy. Together, we can make a difference in the lives of those affected by these mysteries, and your role in this journey is not just valuable, but integral.

Thank you for joining me on this exploration of Dorothy Arnold's life and disappearance. But this is only the beginning. The *Shadows of the Past* series will continue to unravel more historical mysteries, each one a testament to the human spirit and our desire for understanding. In the next book, *The Silent Witness: The Unsolved Murder of Mary Rogers*, we will delve into the haunting case of another young woman whose life was tragically cut short. Just as we've walked alongside Dorothy through the streets of New York, we will now step into the world of Mary Rogers and the mystery that surrounds her unsolved murder.

Together, let's keep searching for the truth, honoring those who disappeared, and supporting those left behind. In the end, Dorothy Arnold's story is a reflection of our shared humanity—the search for meaning in the face of uncertainty and the enduring hope that one day, the shadows will lift, revealing the light of understanding.

EPILOGUE

As we delve into the mystery of Dorothy Arnold's disappearance, it's thought-provoking to imagine how a case like this would unfold in the modern era. The advancements in forensic science, including DNA analysis, surveillance technology, and digital tracking, would undoubtedly provide today's investigators with more tools to solve such a case. Dorothy's fate, one of the most enigmatic unsolved cases of the early 20th century, is a stark reminder of the societal and technological limitations of her time. This tragic story also serves as a poignant reminder of the significant strides we've made in the field of criminal investigation and the evolution of societal norms, particularly in the context of women's roles and freedoms.

EXPERT COMMENTARY

Dr. Julian Hartley, a criminologist specializing in historical cases, points out that cases like Dorothy's disappearance underscore the limited resources available in early 20th-century investigations. He remarks, 'At that time, even basic forensic techniques were in their infancy. It is a testament to both the era's limitations and society's fascination with mystery that cases like Dorothy's remain unresolved today.' Similarly, historian Lisa Grant highlights, 'Dorothy's story is not just about an individual but also about the social dynamics of the period. Her disappearance vividly illustrates the societal pressures faced by women who dared to aspire for *more than the roles assigned to them by their families and society.'*

DISCUSSION QUESTIONS FOR THE VANISHING HEIRESS: THE UNSOLVED DISAPPEARANCE OF DOROTHY ARNOLD

1. **The Complex World of Dorothy Arnold**
   - How did the societal pressures, particularly those related to gender and social status, of being a young woman in early 20th-century New York affect Dorothy Arnold's life? Do you think her social standing as a member of the affluent Arnold family helped or hindered her ability to pursue her ambitions?
   - Dorothy had aspirations to be a writer, but her family viewed this goal as unrealistic. How did the social expectations of her class shape her family's reaction to her ambitions? Do you think Dorothy would have faced the same obstacles today?
2. **Family Dynamics and Secrecy**
   - The Arnold family, particularly her father Francis, was deeply concerned about protecting their social reputation. How do you think this emphasis on secrecy and social standing impacted the investigation into Dorothy's disappearance?
   - How does Elsie Arnold's role within the family, especially her close relationship with Dorothy, offer deeper insight into the dynamics of the Arnold family? What emotions or

conflicts might Elsie have been dealing with after Dorothy's disappearance?

3. **Media Sensationalism and Public Perception**
   - The media frenzy surrounding Dorothy's disappearance played a significant role in shaping the public's view of the case. How do you think media coverage, particularly its sensationalized nature, influenced the investigation, and what parallels can you draw between media involvement in this case and how the media covers high-profile cases today?
   - Discuss the role of "yellow journalism" in Dorothy's case. How did sensationalized reporting contribute to the spread of misinformation, and what were the consequences of this?

4. **Unsolved Mysteries and Theories**
   - Throughout the book, several theories are presented, including the botched abortion theory, abduction, suicide, and voluntary disappearance. Which theory do you find the most plausible, and why? What pieces of evidence, or lack thereof, support your perspective?
   - How did the lack of modern forensic methods impact the investigation into Dorothy's disappearance? How do you think the case would have been handled differently with today's technology?

5. **Emotional and Psychological Toll**
   - The book delves into the emotional toll Dorothy's disappearance exacted on her family, particularly on her sister Elsie and her parents. How does the concept of 'ambiguous loss' manifest in the Arnold family's experience? How might this unresolved grief differ from families who lose loved ones under more conclusive circumstances?
   - How did Dorothy's disappearance affect the public at large? Do you think people outside of the Arnold family were emotionally invested in her case due to her status, or was it simply a fascination with the mystery?

6. **Societal Expectations and Gender Roles**

- How do you think the rigid expectations placed on women of Dorothy's social class influenced her actions and potentially her disappearance? Do you think she was trying to escape those expectations?
- Compare Dorothy's experiences with those of other women in the book, including women of different social standings. How did societal expectations vary based on class, and how might this have impacted Dorothy's choices and eventual fate?

7. **The Role of Family Wealth in the Investigation**
   - The Arnold family's wealth, a significant factor in the investigation, allowed them to hire private detectives and control much of the narrative surrounding Dorothy's disappearance. How do you think their social status affected the investigation? Did it help or hinder the search for Dorothy?
   - What do you think would have been different if Dorothy came from a less affluent family? Would her case have received the same amount of attention, or would it have been treated differently by the media and investigators?

8. **Historical Context**
   - How did the time period in which Dorothy lived—the Gilded Age—shape her life and disappearance? Discuss how the cultural norms of the era, including attitudes toward women, wealth, and status, are reflected in the book.
   - Compare the methods of investigation in Dorothy Arnold's case to how a similar case might be handled today. What are some of the key advancements that would have made a difference in solving her disappearance?

9. **Legacy and Enduring Mystery**
   - Despite the various theories, Dorothy Arnold's disappearance remains a compelling mystery, captivating people more than a century later. What is it about unsolved mysteries that draws us in?
   - How do you think Dorothy Arnold's story contributes to the broader conversation about how we view historical true

crime cases? Does knowing that this case is still unresolved affect your perception of justice and closure?

10. **The Next Chapter in *Shadows of the Past***
    - This book is the first in the *Shadows of the Past* series. In the next book, *The Silent Witness: The Unsolved Murder of Mary Rogers*, another high-society mystery unfolds. Based on what you've learned about Dorothy Arnold's disappearance, what themes or questions do you anticipate being addressed in the next book? What aspects of high-society life or historical investigation do you expect will carry over?

REFERENCES

- Arnold, F. (n.d.). *Frank Arnold*. Retrieved from https://www.arnoldventures.org/people/frank-arnold
- Greenwood, J. T. (n.d.). *The Gilded Age: A History in Documents*.
- National Geographic. (n.d.). The missing heiress at the center of New York's oldest cold case. Retrieved from https://www.nationalgeographic.com/premium/article/dorothy-arnold-missing-heiress-cold-case
- Oxford Research Encyclopedias. (n.d.). *New Women in Early 20th-Century America*. Retrieved from https://oxfordre.com/americanhistory/display/10.1093/acrefore/9780199329175.001.0001/acrefore-9780199329175-e-427
- See Old NYC. (n.d.). New York City in the 1910s: A Decade of Change and Growth. Retrieved from https://seeoldnyc.com/new-york-city-1910s/
- Campbell, W. J. (n.d.). *Yellow Journalism: Puncturing the Myths Defining the Legacies*.
- Collins, P. (n.d.). *The Murder of the Century: The Gilded Age Crime That Scandalized a City & Sparked the Tabloid Wars*.
- Douglas, J. E., & Olshaker, M. (n.d.). *The Cases That Haunt Us*.
- Larson, E. (n.d.). *The Devil in the White City: Murder Magic and Madness at the Fair That Changed America*.
- McDermid, V. (n.d.). *Forensics: The Anatomy of Crime*.
- What Happened to Dorothy Arnold? N.Y. Socialite's 1910 ... Retrieved from https://people.com/dorothy-arnold-missing-persons-case-new-york-socialite-vanished-8662474
- The Gilded Age: The Heyday of High Society Tour NYC. Retrieved from https://newyorkhistoricaltours.com/tour/the-gilded-age-heyday-of-high-society-nyc/
- Frank Arnold. Retrieved from https://www.arnoldventures.org/people/frank-arnold
- New Women in Early 20th-Century America. Retrieved from https://oxfordre.com/americanhistory/display/10.1093/acrefore/9780199329175.001.0001/acrefore-9780199329175-e-427?d=%2F10.1093%2Facrefore%2F9780199329175.001.0001%2Facrefore-9780199329175-e-427&p=emailAwuYQ8TSwIiQ6
- Disappearance of Dorothy Arnold. Retrieved from https://en.wikipedia.org/wiki/Disappearance_of_Dorothy_Arnold
- New York City in the 1910s: A Decade of Change and Growth. Retrieved from https://seeoldnyc.com/new-york-city-1910s/
- Allan Pinkerton's Detective Agency | American Experience. Retrieved from https://www.pbs.org/wgbh/americanexperience/features/james-agency/
- The missing heiress at the center of New York's oldest cold case. Retrieved from https://www.nationalgeographic.com/premium/article/dorothy-arnold-missing-heiress-cold-case

- 10 Things You May Not Know About the Pinkertons. Retrieved from https://www.history.com/news/10-things-you-may-not-know-about-the-pinkertons
- The New York Times "Yellow" Journalism and the Criminal. Retrieved from https://scholars.law.unlv.edu/cgi/viewcontent.cgi?article=1107&context=nlj
- William Randolph Hearst - Crucible of Empire. Retrieved from https://www.pbs.org/crucible/bio_hearst.html
- The Influence of Gender Stereotypes on Crime in Early. Retrieved from https://www.kleiohistoricaljournal.com/post/the-influence-of-gender-stereotypes-on-crime-in-early-modern-europe
- A Timeline of Abortion Law in the United States. Retrieved from https://penncapital-star.com/briefs/a-timeline-of-abortion-law-in-the-united-states/
- History of Private Investigators. Retrieved from https://revealpi.com/blog/person-tracing/the-history-of-private-investigators/
- Families of the Missing: Psychosocial Effects and Therapeutic. Retrieved from https://international-review.icrc.org/sites/default/files/irrc_99_905_4.pdf
- Trials of the Century: 1900 to 1950 | Headlines & Heroes. Retrieved from https://blogs.loc.gov/headlinesandheroes/2020/09/trials-of-the-century-1900-to-1950/
- Evolution of Investigative Techniques: A Journey Through. Retrieved from https://blog.mcafeeinstitute.com/articles/ancient-sleuths-to-modern-detectives-the-evolution-of-investigation-techniques
- Pinkerton's National Detective Agency Records. Retrieved from https://hdl.loc.gov/loc.mss/eadmss.ms003007.3
- 10 Modern Forensic Technologies Used Today. Retrieved from https://www.forensicscolleges.com/blog/resources/10-modern-forensic-science-technologies
- 35 Facts About Dorothy Arnold. Retrieved from https://facts.net/history/people/35-facts-about-dorothy-arnold/
- Police and Crime in the American City 1800–2020. Retrieved from https://oxfordre.com/americanhistory/display/10.1093/acrefore/9780199329175.001.0001/acrefore-9780199329175-e-56?p=emailAYJZPZNe9MiJo&d=/10.1093/acrefore/9780199329175.001.0001/acrefore-9780199329175-e-56
- OVERVIEW AND FINDINGS FROM THE RELIGIOUS. Retrieved from https://www.ncbi.nlm.nih.gov/pmc/articles/PMC3409291/
- Police Responses to Cold and Long-Term Missing Person Cases. Retrieved from https://www.tandfonline.com/doi/full/10.1080/01924036.2022.2094433
- The 100-Year Mystery of Missing Perfume Heiress Dorothy. Retrieved from https://www.thedailybeast.com/the-100-year-mystery-of-missing-perfume-heiress-dorothy-arnold
- Top 10 Bloody 20th-Century Mysteries We'll Probably. Retrieved from https://listverse.com/2017/05/03/top-10-bloody-20th-century-mysteries-well-probably-never-solve/
- The Impact of Media on Public Perception of Crime and the. Retrieved from https://www.silvalegal.com/the-impact-of-media-on-public-perception-of-crime-and-the-criminal-justice-system/

- Sick and Grieving: The Toll of Unsolved Murders. Retrieved from https://collective.coloradotrust.org/stories/sick-and-grieving-the-toll-of-unsolved-murders/
- The Gilded Age: A History in Documents by Janette Thomas Greenwood.
- The Age of Innocence by Edith Wharton.
- High Society: The Life of Grace Kelly by Donald.
- American Heiress: The Wild Saga of the Kidnapping Crimes and Trial of Patty Hearst by Jeffrey Toobin.
- "Social Stratification and Class in the Gilded Age."
- The Devil in the White City: Murder Magic and Madness at the Fair That Changed America by Erik Larson.
- Forensics: The Anatomy of Crime by Val McDermid.
- The Cases That Haunt Us by John E. Douglas and Mark Olshaker.
- Yellow Journalism: Puncturing the Myths Defining the Legacies by W. Joseph Campbell.
- The Murder of the Century: The Gilded Age Crime That Scandalized a City & Sparked the Tabloid Wars by Paul Collins.
- "The Impact of Yellow Journalism on Public Perception."
- Gone: A Girl a Violin a Life Unstrung by Min Kym.
- Family Secrets: The Things We Tried to Hide by Deborah Cohen.
- The Anatomy of Disappearance by Hisham Matar.

ABOUT THE AUTHOR
ELIZA HAWTHORNE

Eliza Hawthorne is a historian, writer, and relentless seeker of the past's darkest secrets. Her particular fascination with unsolved cases from the early 20th century has driven her to dedicate her career to uncovering stories that history tried to leave behind. Her work, a blend of rigorous research and a passion for storytelling, breathes new life into the forgotten and unresolved mysteries of yesteryear.

Eliza's *Shadows of the Past* series doesn't just tell stories; it invites readers to step back in time and experience these unsolved cases firsthand. Each book meticulously reconstructs the circumstances surrounding these chilling cold cases, exploring the facts and cultural and social landscapes of the times. Through meticulous research and captivating narrative, Eliza brings the bustling streets of 1910s New York and the quiet, eerie Midwest to life.

While little is known about Eliza's personal life, her dedication to uncovering hidden truths is unmistakable. She is a private person, preferring to let her work speak for itself. Her work speaks to a deep fascination with the power of secrets, the fragility of memory, and the enduring allure of mysteries that defy explanation. Some speculate that Eliza has spent time traveling to archives, libraries, and even abandoned locations tied to the cases she explores. Perhaps it is this hands-on approach that brings a sense of authenticity to her work, allowing readers to feel as though they are on the hunt for answers alongside her.

Eliza's approach is not just scholarly; it's deeply human. She doesn't just chronicle events; she brings the people involved to life—the victims, the suspects, the investigators, and the communities who lived in the shadow of these crimes. Her books often include new theories and insights drawn from her own investigations, challenging readers to reconsider long-standing assumptions and look at the cases with fresh eyes.

For Eliza, the past is never fully gone; it lives on in the stories she tells and the mysteries she unravels. Through her *Shadows of the Past* series, she offers readers a chance to walk the fine line between history and mystery, fact and speculation, and to immerse themselves in the haunting allure of the unknown.

When she's not writing, Eliza can often be found wandering through dusty archives, sifting through old newspaper clippings, and connecting the dots of history's forgotten puzzles. Her work is an invitation to all who share her passion for the enigmatic and unresolved—an opportunity to step into the past and follow the trail wherever it may lead.

ALSO BY ELIZA HAWTHORNE

SHADOWS OF THE PAST SERIES

- THE VANISHING HEIRESS: THE UNSOLVED DISAPPEARANCE OF DOROTHY ARNOLD
- THE SILENT WITNESS: THE UNSOLVED MURDER OF MARY ROGERS
- WHISPERS FROM THE MURDER FARM: THE CASE OF BELLE GUNNESS: INSIDE THE MIND OF AMERICA'S DARKEST FEMME FATALE

ALSO BY PUBLISHER CORDOVA CONSULTING
AUTHOR - KIMBERLY BURK CORDOVA

LEADERSHIP SERIES

- Turning Chaos into Gold: The Alchemy of Women's Leadership
- The Emotional Intelligence Advantage: Transform Your Life, Relationships, and Career

TRAVEL SERIES

- Santa Fe Uncovered: A Local's Insight into the Heart of New Mexico
- Santa Fe: A Local's Enchanting Journey Through the City Different
- Denver Dossier: Themed Adventures for Every Traveler

EMPOWERING SMALL BUSINESSES SERIES

- Artificial Intelligence Unleashed: An Entrepreneur's Guide to Innovation
- Augmented and Virtual Reality: Unlocking Business Potential for Entrepreneurs

- Cybersecurity for Entrepreneurs: Safeguarding Your Business from Online Threats
- The Entrepreneur's Edge: A 3-Book Compilation on AI, Cybersecurity, and AR/VR